# SOMETIMES
# TO BE NORMAL

## Finding Motivation In Midlife

# Adam Senex

### The Sky is Not the Limit…. The Mind is.

NEW
THINKING
ALLOWED

" In a world in which most of us are preoccupied with externals –
accumulating more stuff and building fake personas to fit every
situation. I consider my task with my books to be as a messenger,
someone that gives myself and others a gentle poke and to suggest
that maybe there are other ways to think about things and more
questions that need to be discovered and asked. Leading to yet
more questions.

My task is to create an interesting, healing and pleasurable art out
of self-examination and ultimately self-realization. This awareness
made available to people who, like me, are finding themselves
caught in the rigors and realizations involved in the process of
growing up as mature adults in the second part of life, having
assumed it would all get easier and that we were the finished
article.  Having no guide and holding ourselves and significant
others to blame for being conned into believing we are fully matured
but in no way prepared for what lies before us in the second part of
life. Or for that matter what goes on behind our backs. If I can only
manage to persuade one other person to look at what may really be
going on in the world and inside of our hearts and minds, then I will
have done tremendously well."

# Adam Senex

MANY THANKS
Adam Sener
x

# Contents

#  Prologue

This book as with all of my books is me doing the best I can with where I am in my life at this moment. It is hopefully a progressive process that can be traced from Getting Better series book 1 and even before with The Great Body Bible under the pen name of The Fitness Wizards and with an assortment of books under the name Gary Walsh. When you read this I will be moving along on my next book. I am still dazed and confused, a little more Zen than rebel nowadays and have I found a comfortable life space somewhere in the middle of my cheeky heroes and chilled demons. I have faith that you will find something within these pages that will help and motivate you to get better in your life. Ultimately that is why we are here, to discover what we are and to transcend what came before at the same time raising the loving energy of this beautiful planet.

It is a glorious sunny February day in the hills that are on the edge of the town close to where I live in the UK. Yesterday whilst I was out walking my 3 dogs I decided I would write this entire book outside in my nature study. This weather reinforces for me that I have made the right decision. I will never know how I would have felt if it had been a snow storm this morning as it could have been in February in the UK. It is a good omen to begin but I am under no illusions as to the weather I may experience between now and finishing this volume. At this time, I do intend to make this a habit, to write at least a few times a week out in nature. This is the UK and we get our fair share of wind and rain, exactly the conditions that would stop me as I can't write in a soggy notebook.

Why did I decide to write outside in the hills?

The first thing is that I do stuff like that all of the time. My world is ever changing. I always have something going on in my head that causes change. Apart from that, the fact is that I will never win any awards for my technical ability or correct use of grammar and my style (at least I have one) has been described as chatty and self-deprecating. A critique I may have just proven with my last comments. I feel both are strengths and weaknesses and as such I aim to make the most of what I am good at. To be honest the way I write is as natural to me as talking and I don't aim to change anytime soon. I do write with passion, soul and a tinge of fear. I like to think that in any creative pursuit there are perfectly good non-conformist ways to communicate to others and for me that happens to be through writing. As the rather dubious saying goes "there is more than one way to skin a cat". What a strange term that has really caught on. I have to wonder at how someone discovered the many ways to skin cats. I am writing outside because that is where I feel at my most soulful and reflective. What better inspiration for any creative pursuit than birdsong? And the dogs get to be outside where they love to be rather than under my desk in their three beds (big desk).

I feel my purpose in writing is to raise awareness generally for both myself and others. This in turn leads to personal progress and to getting better. Getting better in some aspect of life or another is the most common wish expressed to me in my life coaching business. Which is why I concentrate my efforts on how we can all get better. Starting with myself (where else would I start?). We all improve in our own unique ways. Some of us are strong in fitness and nutrition for instance but maybe weak in relationships or feel spiritually lost.

For others it may be totally the opposite. We all have something to work at.

As mentioned I write from my own personal perspective as that is all that I know and that changes daily with my life experience and constant study (which I enjoy so much it makes my toes curl, nerdy I know). The process is ongoing.

In the getting better series I have started to use quotes, images and some cartoons to help the scanners amongst us that thrive on visual stimulation and are phased by page after page of text. And I have found that some good words at the right time go a long way to creating positive memes and overwrite those negative mind viruses that we have all been infected with. I discuss memes further on. I have received good feedback. I follow no blueprint on how to write and my layout can be quite random. I write as I speak with passion and spontaneity. Whether you have read my first three Adam Senex books or any Gary Walsh or The Fitness Wizards books or are just beginning here I have faith in my ability to motivate thoughts and a desire to change ourselves and our environments. My writing in many ways mirrors my behaviour and can best be described as quirky.

I have chosen the pen name Adam Senex simply because my real name Gary Walsh .com was not available. I chose Adam as the story of the first conscious man. I feel our problems all stem from not being fully conscious and it is our biggest challenge in the 21st century both to be aware ourselves and to help the next generation to avoid getting lost in a world of attachment and distraction. I chose Senex from the wise old man archetype as I love Jungian psychology (other psychologies are available) and it seemed to fit me as well as any label ever fits any person (not very well). Strictly speaking though I am probably more the opposite, puer aeternus (eternal boy) than senex (wise old man) but that is another story. However, I do feel my puer may tip that particular balance despite outward appearances. More for the expanding list.

My life journey (corny I know) after becoming more aware as a result of desperation and suffering is depicted in my books and I will continue with that trend as long as I am able, maybe even getting better at that also. I will add it to the list of areas for progress. I have changed much in the last decade and will always be a work in progress, as will we all. How far that work progresses and how interesting our life becomes is down to each and every one of us. The better we each become, the better the world will become and maybe eventually our malevolent manipulators (bless them) will find another game to replace war.

On this, the first day in my new nature study I came across a lady with a very nervous small dog. She commented that he had had some bad experiences. He was full of fear, bless him. It made me think that how we handle our fears throughout life is what determines the quality of our lives. The quality of his life was spent mainly cowering under his carers legs. I would urge all of us to face our fears and not let fear define the direction of our life journey or bring it to a halt altogether. Fear has in the past frozen me to the point of regressing (Cowering just like the little dog). Nothing should ever get in the way of our progress and there is always a way to keep moving in life, it may need a few body swerves but we always have the answer to our own problems but those solutions may be just out of our conscious awareness. The way to rid ourselves of fear is to go through it. With this in mind and with an understanding that fear is the biggest obstacle to progress, bar none I welcome you all to "Sometimes I pretend to be normal" in which I will attempt to show some of the quirky ways that I deal with being different and how I structure my life to better flow with a new, rapidly developing personal reality. Dealing with the very real fear of being alone and at the same time being with others. If you fear the thought of being ostracised due to not conforming it may help to visualise me sitting on a log at the top of a hill overlooking the town reading my writing out to Jake, Smudge and Zing, my three terriers. Nutty as a fruit cake? Maybe! And that as they say is just the tip of the iceberg.

 **Getting Better**

All men and women are potential philosophers, although for some reason, the task and subsequent title has fallen to men more than to women. Maybe men value their opinions more than women but I hope that is changing with the passing of time. The first task of philosophers is to ask questions, the questions that we all have inside but never seem to ask. The second task is to try to find the answers to these questions. However, since the answers are only partial and they seem to raise yet more questions, philosophy both attracts and annoys us. The third task is to encourage all others to ask questions and seek answers for themselves. It is my hope that this book will seek out the inner philosopher in all of us, encouraging original thought and creativity.

We live in a time when we seem to celebrate dysfunctional misfits and idiots more than any person actually worthy of celebration, and we have celebrity politicians ruling our countries and much of the world. It's a time when appearances and impressive speeches have become more important than any depth of character. Speeches impress and then are forgotten. Merely achieving celebrity status makes you an expert on any subject. Celebrities full of their own self-importance seem to be convinced that they actually do have the one last objective truth on any subject. They act as moral guides for society through the social networking sites and a media network that will actually report any old rubbish any celebrity cares to utter, without prior thought. No sooner do thoughts leave their brains than they are aired to millions. Each thought is genius – not an opinion – the last word. A professional soccer player with a record for gratuitous violence is suddenly quoting Aristotle. Interesting. Another spokesperson for kicking racism out of football calls a fellow professional a racist name on the back of a very public court case. Why? Just because he didn't share his views! He dared to have his own opinion. He liked different thoughts. The professional as a role model? With millions of followers?

All things considered, I thought. Yes, that is what I do quite a lot. I think – in fact, I can't seem to stop thinking. How unique might it be for somebody not seeking celebrity status, someone having opted out as much as possible, to offer my unique individual opinions, thoughts, beliefs, and ideas on a wide-ranging and random set of topics, relevant to and affecting us all. Me, a Mr Nobody, voluntarily living life as lightly and invisibly as possible. This book presented here and now for your information could be considered either the ranting of a madman or the wisdom of a life-tortured old sage, depending on your unique interpretation and individual perspective of its contents. More probably, you will see it as just thoughts, opinions, beliefs, and ideas to get your mind juices flowing before free thought becomes illegal, taxable, or we are distracted to such a degree that we entirely lose the ability to personally reflect. Or, in the worst possible scenario, until original thought becomes a skill that humans are no longer capable of performing. Future generations will evolve without such creative ability – unless, of course, we can do it in 140 characters or less! Before you even try it, I am sure a well-known professional sportsman has already tweeted the meaning of life. Think on. Enjoy the currently free process of personal reflection.

The great mind Michel Foucault considers writing about yourself to be what he terms a technology of the self. Writing is used as a tool to say and discover something about yourself in such a way that you could become different. Forms of personal and private writing bring us close to a type of knowledge that transforms us. Through personal writings about ourselves, we produce new ways of being. Through the writing, we practise a freedom to be a different self. This freedom transforms us and grants us power to pronounce truths about ourselves that may lead others to transform themselves. I write, and will continue to write, in order to reinforce new beliefs and to become different. By becoming different, I practise a transformative freedom, which I hope will lead others to find freedom and also change, be it a little or a lot. I guess you could say that I agree with Michel Foucault, a great mind, who for me has hit the nail on the head.

It is my hope that within my ramblings a person will find at least one nugget (hopefully more!) that will help give more meaning to his or her world, meaning at the level at which most of us live, on the ground, in the real world, and not with our heads in the clouds. In this book I will discuss how I try to live my philosophy from day to day. I am not entirely sure what my philosophy is, and I am changing daily. I never really succeed 100 per cent in my aims, but I am mindful of much that I had never even been aware of previously in my life. The structure will be quite random, as that is how life and thoughts arrive with me, how I reflect on them and thus develop my reflections. I have yet to learn how to think in nice, ordered chapters.

Much has been written about the flow of the universe; well, I consider that is how I write. An idea presents itself when the time is right. There follow many random thoughts and ideas for me to ingest. First, I would like to introduce both myself, Julie, my wife, the dogs and my turbulent past, and then we will enter the random world of my daily thought processes. You may think it self-indulgent to talk about oneself in a book, but I hope the following arguments will help state my case. I can only view the world from my unique perspective; attempting anything else would be foolhardy.

Existentialist philosophy argues that when you ask about the meaning of life or existence, you are really asking about the nature of active, participatory existence. You want to know what the significance is of your way of existing that is different from others'. You have no way to detach from your own participation with existence, so you should approach and understand your existence through an analysis of how living itself happens or what it is like to be an active participator (Detmer, 2008).

Nietzsche rejects the notion of a right way to see things. He sees no objective truth in the world to be discovered. Instead, he thinks you must understand the world through your perspective, one that always reflects your own specific interests. He thinks there are no facts, just interpretations. His view is called perspectivism, the view that all descriptions of the world are given from a biased or self-interested point of view. Furthermore, although you hold at any given moment a given perspective, you're never reducible to that perspective. Your identity is never fixed; new perspectives are always possible for you (Cox, 2009).

One of the key aims of this book is to provide all of this in an easy-to-read, easy to understand style. I have found that often (not always) academic writing can be difficult or impossible to understand. I do not consider myself an academic. Labelling and being labelled is one of my pet hates, but it's difficult to avoid. Academics' discourse gives them power over others who are not as proficient in the discourse, and so they maintain a hierarchy which keeps them in an elevated position. By using their own language, or a version of the same language, they effectively exclude many of us who might benefit from their learned message. I hope to bridge the gap, thus providing a more readable access to some of the ideas of the great thinkers, while I have a foot in both camps. Is that allowed? It's probably not encouraged, but the writer of a book based on individualism has to take the chance not to conform if the end looks to justify the means. I am sure I will get crucified from all sides. It is so easy to criticise.

> *At no point do I claim any special mastery over how to live life, but I am committed to finding a formula through experience that could assure a person some success.*

> —Benjamin Franklin

This book is not a typical self-help book. My principal wish is to inspire thought, create unrest, disturb sleep and contribute some broader perspective than what is immediately on offer, waiting to be plucked ready made from the limited choice available on the society opinions shelf.

I will not inform you how to discover God, find the partner of your dreams or how to make friends and influence others. That is your personal calling not mine. I respect your potential to create perhaps more than you do. I know you will not avoid all of life's experiences, temptations and distractions surround you, and that fear and pressure to conform to norms weaken your soul and diminish your progress.

I believe that for you to progress you will have to become more responsible than your conformist nature wishes you to be. I acknowledge the monumental significance of spirituality in this undertaking and of claiming back your life and becoming more

11

whole. I affirm no particular belief for you to adopt. Again, that is your calling.

This book is based on a personal and ongoing journey as I began with "Dazed and Confused', 'More Rebel than Zen' & 'Chilled Demons & Cheeky Heroes'. The progress made between the four books is marked. My writing style has been described as self-deprecating and chatty. I prefer to think I write to you as I might talk to you if we meet, clearly, respectfully and passionately. Always challenging you to find your answers to the ongoing questions that your life asks of you. Your journey is uniquely your journey, not someone else's. It is never the wrong time to start. The best time is always now.

I wish to suggest that all books help us become more than we are when we begin to read them. I will even go as far as to state that if a book is not going to help then we should not be reading it. However, that is not likely as even the mindful behaviour of focusing on reading for a reasonable amount of time helps our minds. In the last few years I have mentored young men that could not even get past the first page in any book. They lacked the attention span. A common occurrence in the 21st century.

Even the resistance to certain words contained in books holds a valuable lesson. For me the word God was guaranteed to have me stop reading any book as being too religious. Then I realised that my conditioning, that religious people were a bit 'special' and not in a good way had blocked my learning and ability to formulate my own thoughts, ideas and opinions. I was narrow minded when it came to religion. I had been brainwashed to believe what others wanted me to believe. I have since expanded my awareness and I have even developed my own personal concept of God and world view in general, which is more an acceptance of never being able to truly know, as any God that words can describe cannot be God. Let's face it we are all pretty clueless but have an inkling and that may be all we need. More importantly I have a much more open mind and love to allow others their own thoughts also. This can be true in many areas. If resistance is felt, there is a lesson to learn. I am now willing to learn and hold no views that are so fixed that they may never change.

My point is that this book is a self-help book, as they all are. It is the aim of this book to help all readers to progress. There are many areas for getting better, so many that I feel I can't fail in my aim for all readers to progress in some way from the experience of reading this book.

I aim to relate quite complex ideas in an easy to read and understand format that bridges the gap between academic work and mainstream texts.

I will use personal anecdotes to make the theories become real for you. Everything contained in this book we are living in every moment. That is an important lesson, I am writing about your life and my life. The ability for you to relate the contents of this book to yourself is vital to your progress and mine. And in fact vital to any learning process. Life is a learning process. We are learning to become whole. What that means will become about as clear as mud in this book.

As the person choosing to read this book you are in a constant process of change. The aim of this book is to help you ensure that the changes you experience are progressive. The act of reading this book or any other such book ensures that a different you will put the book down than the you that picked it up to begin reading in the first place. All books change your life, it is my aim that this book will have a profound effect on every reader and that your state of mind will become one of progress in each and every aspect of your existence.

 If this book were to have a research question, it would be as follows:

How might we learn to master the art of personal progression in order to create peace of mind and heart, give meaning to, and shape the direction of our lives for the benefit of our souls, the planet and mankind?

The scope of the subject is colossal, however my aim is simple, to guide my readers, my clients and myself to a life of progression. A life full of meaning and a life to be lived to the full until we eventually and predictably arrive at the bridge into the unknown. For now, we can only live the lives we know we have. We have a finite timescale barring any abrupt endings. Life is unpredictable so we best get on with it. Nobody really knows past 'lights out' what the future holds. It would be pointless and a terrible waste of time not to live for this time whilst banking on immortality. We can live well and progress right now and if there turns out to be continued consciousness for humans past physical death then I believe that is called a win-win situation. There is no place for narrow mindedness or resistance to personal change. We have to be as receptive to change in ourselves as we seem to be to new technology. If the new technology amazes you? You are in for a rare treat once you begin to understand what you might be capable of. The new you is far more impressive than the latest model of any chosen gadget.

Change is inevitable. Human beings and much of life on earth are evolving and changing more rapidly than ever before. There are two rules for readiness and acceptance of change, keep an open mind and make the change progressive whenever there is personal choice involved.  We are learning that we have more control over who we are than we ever dreamt possible. True enough, there are barricades to turn into bridges but they become bridges all too easily once the awareness, belief and expectations become great and the old myths have been exploded.

The hardest task is probably understanding what we are at this moment in time:

How did we become this self?

What are the forces that have determined who we are and can we break free from these forces?

Can we really become anything we want to be?

Can we become whole, sacred, enlightened, saved, a higher self, authentic or any of the other terms used to describe a human being making progress beyond the rigid and widely accepted norms?

Are you happy being the norm, the same as other norms?

I have personal answers for all of these questions and the outlook is very good.  You can develop your own. I am not saying it will be easy, however the human race has many problems caused by fragmented psyches, cultural conditioning and our selfish genes. All of these can be overcome. Now more than ever before, we are capable of transcending our nature, cultural conditioning and mastering our psyches in order to take the human race onto a new level of development. The answer to all of them is to be found inside of us. By each of us becoming all we can be, the human collective will become all that it can be. As the saying goes - if you want to change the world then start with yourself. Fairy steps will get the job done. Impatience will not. The human race is on the move, both getting worse and better and we are all involved. Our choices can determine the future of this planet or at least the length of our stay on this planet. The planet can go on long after we as a species have screwed up.

This is not even taking into account the amazing possibilities being discovered within Quantum physics and the afterlife experiments. That changed beliefs may take a while longer to filter through the archaic and fearful resistance to change, but when it comes Human beings may become super beings compared to what we are today. 100 years is not long for so much radical change and the changes and discoveries are most definitely that. The future of the human race is so finely balanced; we could become extinct in record time or accelerate into a new era. And that future either way is in our hands, minds and hearts. Each and every one of us has a duty to leave a legacy of progressing as far as we can before we check out. Memories and behaviours last far longer than material objects.

16

Getting better until the day we die. It couldn't be simpler. All the best ideas are simple. Even dying is a mystery tour. Nobody knows what that journey into the unknown holds in store for us but I am very well read and the knowledge and wisdom I have gained leaves me more optimistic than ever. Reading has given me a world view that is far more optimistic than I could possibly obtain from the media, science, second hand religions and acceptance of conformist views of how the world is and how it might be in our imagined futures.

This book will provide signposts for that positive change that I will be calling progress. All we need to ensure is that we choose progress each time we get a choice, however small the choice may seem and eventually the snowball effect will change the world via memes and actual physical change to our brains. We will be happier, more understanding and tolerant of others differences and the world will become a better place. The opposite is also possible and can be witnessed daily in the media and all around us. The race is on, maybe whoever coined the phrase the human race knew that it would all come down to a good versus evil scenario at the end of the day.

What exactly does progress entail and in what areas can we progress?

Improved awareness - More curious - More knowledge – Better listening - Improved self-image - Better nutrition – New attention for life lessons – Loving relationships – Fitter body - Better understanding - New jobs – New opportunities – New adventures everyday – Less addictions & attachments – Less depression & anxiety – Less fear - Less anger - and on.......>

In short we can progress in every aspect of our lives, every day and in as yet undiscovered ways. We are experts in getting better, all we need is to just get in the spirit of progress. Once immersed we can't fail to improve our lives and touch all others that we come into contact with. A win-win situation. Every choice can either diminish us or expand us.

There is so much progress to make. I could fill the book with areas for progress. Progress includes anything that you want it to include. Now that is a lot of choices and a life packed full of progress and motivation.

All we have to do is improve ourselves, now that isn't too much to ask. And while we reap the personal benefits of a better life we are all impacting the planet in one big progressive high energy tidal wave.

> *"Before beginning a Hunt, it is wise to ask someone what you are looking for before you begin looking for it............You can't always sit in your corner of the forest and wait for people to come to you... you have to go to them sometimes."*
>
> - Pooh Bear

You have begun to look. I am here to tell you what to look for and the rest is up to you. Happy hunting.

Life is a process and our life purpose is to progress throughout the process as we live it or as forces dictate we live it.  This life purpose could not be simpler but as I mentioned all of the best ideas are simple and have been inside of us all along. So look no further for your life purpose, here it is.

Our life purpose is to progress to wholeness in the process of life, for the betterment of self, others, the planet and beyond. To boldly go where we have not personally been before. SIMPLE!

 ## Sometimes I Pretend to Be Normal

In the real world we are drawn and cajoled into behaving normally by rules and the opinions of others as our guides. I believe that others actual or perceived thoughts about us is probably a more effective powerful method of control and should we find ourselves ostracised or isolated for being different it is a far worse place to be than being punished once or reprimanded for any breach of the rules. Norms are subtle but powerful methods of social control and manipulation as our governments and marketing professionals know only too well.

Once individual awareness nudges us awake and conscious many of the rules and conditioned thoughts (becoming opinions) begin to seem out of step and even a little ridiculous to our new open minded view of the world, we no longer accept our reality blindly as it is handed to us. This is the time that we feel displaced as the need to express alternative points of view and behaviours surfaces in even the most rudimentary interactions and if followed we can seem argumentative or contancrous. No longer accepting of what is normal thought. It begins by feeling that we are being deliberately argumentative with those close to us and others and those close notice because it is a change from what they consider normal for us.

We no longer have a normal. This period is tough. We then feel we should say nothing and grit out teeth. We have tried to convince others there are other world views and failed miserably despite our passion regarding our new awakened state. The interactions are draining. We fail to even scratch the surface and can't see why others don't get it. Even though we were the same only a short while ago. Now, we understand that readiness for change is essential, others have to be looking for answers. Readiness may come at any time or never, so we continue to say nothing and pretend to be normal whilst retaining our ideals and resisting compliant agreement with anything we don't agree with. Saying nothing replaces disagreeing with others and the temptation to preach our current thoughts and ideas. The energy needed for interactions such as these is draining and eventually we resist the meetings and become more selective with who we have in our social group.

This avoidance of others is due to the frustration caused to our newly opened minds and it comes as part of the transition from our old world to the new world that is being attracted by our new thinking. Part of us is dying and in the process of being born anew. Like will attract like and our new world is constantly forming. We have joined a silent minority brimming over with passion for our new discoveries but isolated from others with which to share and expand. We still smile and nod in all the right places and occasionally our passion overcomes us in the moment and we preach something totally alien to others. We feel out of the flow and alone with others. Have we gone insane? This is a tough time. As mentioned, a part of us is dying for a new life to emerge. We are in a transitional period and in fact we will be in a transitional period for the rest of our lives. We are faced with losing everything we have accepted as our lives to this point. I have heard it labelled a cocoon which is very apt description.

We know that progress towards an expanded self is possible, (we feel the pull) but only by relinquishing our former selves and the endless pretence which is a moment like clinging to a cliff by our fingertips, we have to let go and have faith in the process.

The task is to release people, places, careers, attachments, addictions and in fact anything solely ego driven and fake and embrace our new totality – ego- soul and spirit. Intuition and listening to our heart overrides doing "the right thing" according to society and our cultures. If we are lucky we will retain a few true friends and family as they will accept us and maybe eventually understand us. Having dozens of friends is extremely unlikely and there will be precious few, if any institutions that will reflect our new, open minded ever evolving self. There will be no room for antiquated dogmatic beliefs and an ever expanding process of self. Institutions tend to stand still, exactly the opposite is the case for an awakened self.

It is so easy to get stuck in the rut between old life and new life. No longer satisfied with the superficial side of life such as gossiping, mindless television viewing, consumerism, overeating, compulsive drinking, attachments, addictions and many more of the considered norms that now feel strangely unfulfilling and leave us knowing in our depths that there must be more to life. At this point many throw themselves with more gusto into the world of excess of all kinds. I did this and nearly ended up killing myself.

Having relied for so long on our myriad of addictions and distractions we failed to develop alternative personal and social resources. So we continue to play the game by pretending the norms are our norms but all the while we are on the lookout for meaning and others such as ourselves to further reinforce our changes in world view and to motivate us to follow our soul's calling. I have seen people in this process labelled as seekers but personally resist such labels as this life path is uniquely individual and whilst we can and should become knowledgeable about others journeys, there is a danger that we end up following yet another group "norm". This is a rebirth that can only ever be our rebirth.

There is a period in the process when we rebel against our cultural norms and become to quote my book title *more rebel than zen.* At this point our awakened state cause us to raise ourselves above others. We are vocal about our right (non-conformist) thinking and others wrong (conformist) thinking. This attitude is pure ego and must be seen as such, a barrier to our progress. We are all entitled to our thoughts from wherever they come and we are all at different stages in our life process which in any case is different for each of us. It is not possible to change others by ramming our current thoughts down their throats. However, by being the changes, we can illicit original thought that can help others and create a ripple effect of positive change in others that will be totally their choice. Getting better is what we set for ourselves and if our personalities show benefits to our lifestyles and peace of mind then change will ripple throughout our contact base and beyond.

I am learning by trial, error and constant study. In writing this book I have no right way to get better but I do have my way that I believe is making me better than I was. I will share in the pages of my books many quirky lifestyle habits that I have tried or adopted. I say quirky because they are not the norm and in my thinking all that goes against the norm gets me interested.

As with all of my books my attitude is open-minded and I consider our minds to be our only limitation. If we can truly open our hearts and minds life will be very interesting. I use the word interesting in place of happiness because without the opposite of happiness happy would simply not exist and it is within our acceptance of how we deal with the opposite moments to the considered ideals that our whole life experience is formed. We can live an interesting, engaging and meaningful life once we grasp that it is how we perceive our precious moments that creates our world view and shapes our experience as being rewarding or not. Thinking of happy and sad as equally enriching and not to be resisted is a great place to begin. Just accept the moments that we can't change as part and parcel of the way things are and know that they will pass, as will those moments that we love so much. A good life, well lived has much to do with how we balance our opposites. Balancing our cultural and primal created ego self with our deep authentic soul self is the path to getting better and meaning not happiness is the realistic goal for us all. The search has never been for eternal happiness but rather a deep meaningful life and that is within the grasp of us all.

I discuss progress a lot in my books and talks. However, it is not materialistic progress. I am not going to give you tips on how to get rich or how to get a bigger pile of stuff even though much of what I will discuss can lead to an improved life and a better standard of living but as a side effect of becoming more in the flow of life and as such better people, with loving motives seem to be able to create more in their lives by letting go and ultimately changing from the inside promotes outside changes also. By progress I mean progress in human potential, in knowing ourselves and understanding others better. Life is a process that we have lost the ability to work with and rediscovering the art of living is the key to the good life well lived. God, the life force, the universe and my favourite the Tao are names for blueprints for living well and getting back in step. They may vary in interpretation but they are all the same. We have lost our way and are being held captive out of the flow for profit and crowd control and it is the task of each and every one of us to find our way back into the arms of the Tao (substitute your favoured term). Christ, Buddha and Mohammed are examples of the ideal mode of being, there are more and the allegorical message is always the same but we are all just too busy comparing, wanting and having to realise our human potential. That is changing slowly. The question is will it happen before we manage to destroy each other and the planet? The race is on. Progressing to a calmer, kinder and more loving self is where we begin. Reprogramming our minds is the place to work. I will show you much that will help us all to become better people in this book you hold here in your hands. We can move closer to realising our human possibilities. Progress in being alone and in being with others. Progress towards that optimum mode of being exhibited by whatever our culture uses as the ideal, it matters not, moving away from the current trend of having as much as possible and being better than others. A modification of ego fuelled life and an enhancement of soul-self through acceptance of all that we contain. The many faces of God or our psyches. Above all else a progression away from an inauthentic personality and life towards an authentic life lived in the flow. I hope to motivate myself and you to change and then to provide some signposts for you to follow that may help you on the journey. I will begin with discussing normality further and how being normal just might be the less sane option for any human to adopt. Then I will talk about a project that I used when I attended toastmasters in order to balance my introverted tendencies and to be with others more often. I chose the topic of progress for my speech, using an acronym to illustrate how progress is possible for us with relatively few changes other than in the way we think about life and our experience here on this planet. I will then proceed with many of the quirky ways I make my life more interesting and attempt to re-programme my mind and take back my life. Making it more authentically mine by surrounding myself with meaning and finding meaning in everyday objects and situations. Finally, I will share with you some powerful and simple method for changing our thought processes to bring us success as opposed to the negative chit chat that prevails for even the most optimistic of us. The purpose being to prime ourselves for the most interesting and prosperous life possible to us in the time we have available.

 **The Insanity of Normality**

We all tend to be reassured to be thought of as normal. The "norm" is where mental health professionals intend us to be when we undertake to submit to therapy of any kind. If we are not happy, contented and free from neurosis then we are considered as not normal and treated so we can become normal once more with minimal delay. A happy, healthy, normal member of society is the desired label for finding comfort and peace of mind. If we are restless and threatened in this normal world, then there must be something wrong with us. Society normal behaviour is considered sane and behaving otherwise is less then sane and maybe even insane. There are considered normal behaviours in every conceivable area of our lives put there by our ruling classes for profit and control and many other less then sane motives have been suggested. imprinted in our minds at every turn through the media and conditioning framework that works on us throughout our lives. Even upheld by others of our kind through public opinion that is anything but public and also controlled by the aforementioned conditioning machinery that control our minds and does our thinking for us. That ends when we finally wake up to the game being played with our minds behind our backs. The norms are a big part of how we are controlled and control each other. A very subtle but extremely effective control mechanism.

We believe, having been convinced that we live in a normal society and therefore a sane society. If we feel displaced, then we must not be sane and therefore we are crazy. Erich Fromm in his book Sane Society stated a very strong case for neurotic and sensitive types in our society being uncomfortable in a society that is anything but sane when looked at with an open mind. And that the types affected by life on this planet are exhibiting a much saner reaction to the reality of life on earth. A genuine use for the phrase "it's not me it's all them others".

No sane person could be comfortable with what goes on within our societies on this planet. When we are feeling as if we are alone in feeling bad about life and that we must be crazy we would do well to consider my next points and then investigate more what might be occurring behind our backs by reading from the list I will include at the end of all of my books. Making up your own mind.

Sane human beings have slaughtered 100,000,000 of our own species in the last century and I have seen that figure as much as doubled. Whatever the figure there is not a sane explanation for any of this let alone the lies that our governments are expecting us to believe. This slaughter continues somewhere in the world on a daily basis. Often by countries that purport to be good and often for owning arms that these countries themselves supplied to the "evil" ones. The problems are created by our governments and then the solution is also provided and they are always on the side of good and the others are evil. Bullshit! This slaughter is deliberately orchestrated by governments that are never honest about why it is happening. Something smells across our beautiful planet.

At least half of the world's population is starving to death or living in poverty. The other half are greedy to the extreme and spend billions on our greedy needs and then billions more on curing the resulting damage that the greed has caused. We are virtually incapable of a loving relationship for life and it is always the fault of others. Our spiritual values contradict our practical everyday values perfectly we live the opposite life to the one we preach about. We worship false idols. Phones, food, television, computer games, the internet, cars and too many other to mention here. We think more of our stuff, our addictions, our attachments and wanting more than we do of others and of Gaia (the earth as a living organism).

We live in fear of what others think, isolation, dogs, not being good enough and whatever else our oppressors can paint as worthy of fear in the media. We are held in fear at every turn. Every moment in the media I see as an April fool's joke that we all keep falling for endlessly. The news is an endless lying fairy tale designed to control our every thought and action. We naively think that we have a say in how we are governed through our vote. Do you really think that the people have any say in anything in this world that matters? It is all just to keep us distracted and away from asking any real questions or from spending our time better employed at improving ourselves. They want us to think we matter to them. We don't.

We have multiple personas to fit every situation or we are thought of as weird and we think we are being true to ourselves. We are not even sure who we are.

We are influenced by an optimum mode of being as demonstrated by figures such as Christ, Buddha, Mohammed and more but we are more interested in our religion being literal and historical or being better than others than in any true message from the teachings. In reality we live in the opposite world of having and this is considered normal. It makes me laugh to see religious shows by people that are living the opposite life and that they think they are resetting the balance. The contrast in society is stark and so obvious but there are none so blind that will not see. The extremes and narrow minded values of both worlds (practical and religious) seem to be equally destructive. We seem incapable of accepting and balancing opposites. We go from one to the other or remain in one world! But never consider there may be a way to reconcile a middle way.

We must take the time to consider all of this and much more when we aim to get better and live the good life. There are an increasingly aware percentage of our species that are instigating change and even some groups such as the Quakers attempting to progress with the times in a way that might just be one of the answers for some. Only time will tell if such groups can shake off the stigma of the past and move into the future with an improved public image. I for one was very surprised upon reading about the Quakers for the first time to find them very aware of the changing spiritual requirements in modern society. We do not need groups to change but some may be more comfortable being amongst likeminded others. We are already members of the only group we should ever need. Quakers allow their unique worship meetings to be experienced by anyone. If you are curious I recommend you contact them and read some books. I am not a Quaker and have not attended worship but I have read many books and I will always advise any action that shows much promise for personal and spiritual growth free from dogma and dedicated to helping others. It is my intention to experience Quaker worship.

We may be some distance from much I have mentioned in the world but we are responsible for change in our world. Change has to begin with each of us in our hearts and minds and it may entail going against the "norms". In fact, it almost certainly will as many of our normal practices are killing this planet and harming others just like ourselves. And harming each and every one of us. It is a difficult situation and we will never get it right all of the time but we can get better. We just have to make lifestyle choices that will better suit our souls and Gaia. These can be small to begin with and expand as we expand. A good example creates a ripple effect that becomes our legacy well into the future. However long that future may be. We may even be able to change the norms over time to ones that better suit both human beings and the planet.

Do we really value being normal more than being authentic? This may be the first choice. Remembering that just because the majority behave in a certain way does not make it right, just comfortable conformism.

I don't want to appear to think that all normal people are psycho either. There are many normal behaviours that are life enhancing and certainly the opposite exists to all of the negative I have mentioned. I am just trying to make the point that the normal- not normal border is not at all clear cut and that there is much honour in breaking away from the norms if they are not serving us well without all the endless self – recrimination and self-doubt that being outside of the norm can produce. Feeling guilty for being different is just not an option. And in fact I want to suggest that we should feel proud any time we take a stance away from the norms that enhances who we are as authentic and unique human beings. We should be so unique that it becomes very difficult to stick any labels on us or all labels fit but not very well. We have become beyond labelling and as such we are then labelled strange, weird, crazy or quirky and can never be pinned down. The problem is that the behaviours that are mainstream and publicised as if we are proud of them do not enhance humanity. Rarely is our day full of life enhancing messages rather than messages encouraging greed, hostility and conflict. We are being taught to accept it all as normal. Brainwashed into becoming a part of something that we feel neither comfortable with or part of. And taught to blame others that are in exactly the same situation as us of being lied to and convinced that they are on the side of God and right. Are we really that naïve after all of these years of being conned? It would seem that we are but there are signs of change and a growing number of people that know that by changing their lives and thoughts they can change the world. And that the worlds media is the first of their problems and it needs to be shut out in order to not be victim to the continuing onslaught of negative programming bombarding us by way of our "must have" technology. The exact technology that has our rulers knowing everything about us and we actually pay them for the privilege of being spied on constantly. And we queue up for the next and latest version of their spy-tech. Proud to be seen with these devices in our grasp, we are assisting in our own slavery.

Okay! I think it is fair to say I have said enough about being normal for now. It is a state that we are conditioned to adopt. We are imprisoned by our norms. I will end this section with a short anecdote that depicts how this can work in the real world. It happened quite recently at my house. It may highlight the size of the task ahead by seeing that it is prevalent in society in the most intimate places in our lives. This particular incident stars my Mother and the delivery lady and concerns my life-space (home) which I never thought would produce such worrying comments. I will be discussing my life-space later in this book. I stood chatting to a lady that delivers parcels to my house occasionally. The chat landed on the topic of house plants and I put forward my thoughts on plants life which I have touched on in my other books. In summary – my thought is that our energy in our homes combined with our good intentions to the plants contributes to the plants health and that I use my plants health to gauge how in flow and in the moment we are at any given time. There is research by a gentleman called *Backster* backing this up and should be read as it is amazing. My experience has backed up this theory and I have plants that outgrow my living conditions regularly. If the plants in our house are struggling the first place Julie (wife) and I look is to our peace of mind and general feelings of well-being and being present in the now moment. With this said, I invited the lady into my home to see my plants that were the cause of my last house move with their abundant growth.

As we toured my home the lady suddenly exclaimed "Oh! You are one of them, aren't you?" I had no clue what she was talking about as people's relationship with plants has long been a common theme in society. Something she had seen had caused her to pigeon hole me. Noticing her obvious struggle to put into words what "one of them" actually was I tactfully shifted the chat and carried on regardless. I knew that if I probed for what she meant I would not be very polite and I had after all invited her into my home. I smiled to myself after she had left, shocked that a friendly and hospitable gesture could backfire so easily and not all others are as tactful as I am. My Mother beats this as she came to my home for a rare visit for the first time in ages she exclaimed before even making it to the toilet. "Adam! There is a lot of evil in here." I do have some interesting ornaments which I will chat about later but I hardly feel the Spanish inquisition reaction was appropriate. I totally ignored her as anyone trying to be calmer knows our own nearest and dearest are our biggest challenge.

From this we can see that the tendency to label is rife in society and others think it is all right to just open their mouths and let the words fall out. One of the biggest challenges in going against the norms is how to deal with these normal people that surround and judge you at every turn. I just shrug and if I do get the chance I deal with their point in my own time in my own way, that is often enough for them to understand that there are other ways life can be lived and their way is not the only and right way. I used to react with annoyance but I have learned that just plays into their hands and their judgement in their eyes has been accurate and they are of course right about everything because they can easily obtain reinforcement from other normal people. The rule here is to be calm and shrug lovingly. Letting it go as trivial and unimportant. An attitude that our society could well benefit from adopting.

I guess my mother and my delivery friend consider their homes to be normal and mine to be abnormal or deviant. I have messages and teachings throughout my home for myself and for the world that as I like to live in it. You can judge (or not) my quirky home for yourselves later.

Still on the subject of judging and labelling. I have endlessly witnessed people that consider themselves normal uttering the phrase "Live and let live! That is my motto" and with the next breath prove that is not their motto at all. The motto is considered normal but sadly it is also normal not to live up to one's life mottos. It does not take a brain surgeon to witness that in our world there is very little "live and let live" going on.

"LET THE REFINING AND IMPROVING OF YOUR OWN LIFE KEEP YOU SO BUSY THAT YOU HAVE LITTLE TIME TO CRITICIZE OTHERS."

H. JACKSON BROWN, JR.

 **Progress**

Change and impermanence are facts of life and as such are inevitable for us all. Our choices serve to either regress or progress us as human beings. Our purpose in life is therefore clear, to progress and develop by understanding ourselves and our complex roles in our societies. To strip away our fake identities is part of the life process if the choice is to progress. Progress is the only choice for the meaningful life. The life well lived. The courageous choice. Every human being's role in life is to progress and help others to progress in a genuine, loving and compassionate way. All choices come down to progression or regression. To a choice of life or death. Death is coming to us all in good time. Choosing life is the only sensible choice while the choice is available. Choosing progress is choosing life.

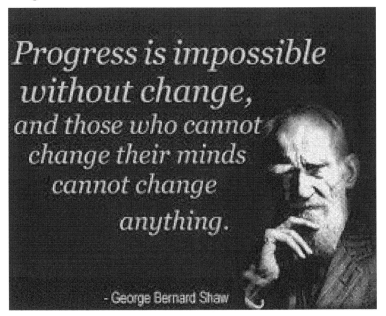

Progress is impossible without change, and those who cannot change their minds cannot change anything.

- George Bernard Shaw

It is not whether we will change or not but whether those changes will be progressive or not is what our life challenges are. Change is always coming. Making it change for life progress is the only thing we are trying to control. Developing each and every facet of our bodies and minds is the best that we can do. Developing our roles in a genuine way as we progress away from our fake personas.

**Think like this** – if today feels like a "get through it" day to you. Change that thought and think. *"I am going to make this a day that I take a giant leap or a fairy step forward, I will do all that I need to do to keep myself moving forward today".*

Improved awareness and acceptance of what can't be changed - More curious and less acceptance of what can be changed - More knowledge + experience = wisdom – Better living environment. More empathetic listening - Improved self-image and life purpose – Better nutrition management – New attention for life lessons from any quarter – Loving relationships with more people – Fitter, healthier, stronger, leaner body – More peace of heart and mind - Happier - Better understanding of others through learning - New and better suited jobs – New life opportunities through greater participation – New adventures everyday – Better sleep patterns.

**Still thinking** - *"So many areas in my life to progress myself and to help others progress also. I have stuff to do in my life to make it even better than it has ever been. I aim to develop every role in my life. Whatever I am doing right now I will do it well and develop my role to the maximum. I say yes to life; progress is my mantra. However, true progress dictates that I know myself better, that I strip away any fake identities and achieve all of this through my becoming a more complete Soul-self."*

How can this become how we approach every day?

Could finding this answer be one route to a much more well balanced and contented life?

A realization that what you read is what you are actually living. Readers too often read and think that the books are about others, basically anyone but them. They are about you, me and all others. Embrace that you are living the learning or you should be. Use your new knowledge and with experience as your guide, wisdom will be yours.

The theme running through this book is personal progress. The intention is that we will all progress in thought and action either a little or a lot due to the experience of reading for you, and for me, writing this book.

Progress in what? You may ask. Anything that leads to a genuine expansion and enhancement of ourselves and others as human organisms. Our health, fitness, wellness, spirituality, understanding, living environment, wisdom, knowledge base and experience for that wisdom, awareness, relations to others, the planet and all of life, self-knowing, self-mastery, a personal belief system, meaning and the list just goes on.

It is my firm belief that personal progress and raising our personal energy level is the purpose and meaning of life. But what is progress and how can we recognize real progress from simple material gains that may even be a sign of regression for the human organism (us)?

I have heard progress described as "choosing life" and regression as "a living death". The point to take note of here is that progress in global technology is not personal progress. Being able to buy increasingly sophisticated gadgets and appliances can reflect either progress or regression for human beings, or even an evolution to a different human being, part machine. Personal progress is more a measure of social relationships, physical health and fitness, spiritual health, mental health and balance and the creation of as near a whole and complete psyche and body as possible for the time on this earth. An organism in harmony with the environment. This may be termed enlightenment or salvation or other such worthy but far off and unreachable terms. I prefer to see it as a caring for the soul or simply getting better. Where this progress can ultimately lead is unknown, no matter what is promised, nobody really knows. As Forest Gump wisely stated "life is like a box of chocolates and you never know what you are going to get". Being on a mystery tour is a great way to live life. One never knows what we will get or what true human potential really is. What we can work on is going to sleep each day having made progress in our lives in one way or another and giving thanks for that fact.

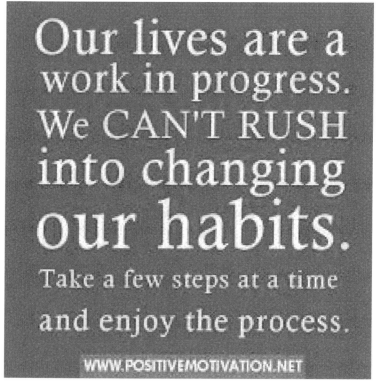

Our lives are a work in progress. We CAN'T RUSH into changing our habits. Take a few steps at a time and enjoy the process.

WWW.POSITIVEMOTIVATION.NET

There are many ways to personal progress in our life process and according to our current mode of knowing our physical death is guaranteed one may as well choose life in the here and now. You may want to explore death and the many theories out there that will help formulate a personal world view for you. This progress is infinitely more rewarding long term and less expensive and as such less exclusive, than amassing big piles of stuff. You don't need great sacks of money to make progress and the beauty is that this progress in no way bars one from attaining material growth and sacks of money. There are many instances including my life where once material growth becomes a more realistic part of a larger life philosophy, befitting a human being's deeper needs and true nature, as opposed to one's sole focus and reason for living, life then supplies all that we need.

So the question is - are you moving forward in your life?

Can you relax at the end of a hard day and give thanks for the progress made in your life as an expanding human being in some detail?

There are times when we are trying to achieve a goal that knowing where to start seems like the biggest barricade since the Great Wall of China. This book you are reading is a great start and I will list some questions that will highlight areas for growth next just to show you there is much we can do to progress each and every day.

# Strive for progress not perfection.

*– unkown*

Don't know where to start progressing? Maybe these questions will help to guide you -

Do you think? Can you stop thinking? Do you look after your brain? Are you expanding spiritually? Are you in control of your emotions? Are you in control of your body? Are you in control of your nutrition? Do you listen with empathy? Are you considerate? Are you kind? Are you loving? Are you generous? Are you peaceful? Are you compassionate? Are you forgiving? Is your knowledge base increasing? Do you read challenging books? Are you becoming wiser (knowledge x experience)? Can you honestly say you know yourself? Do you really know others? Do you read, write and reflect (journal)? Do you assume responsibility for your life? Do you work to align your shadow with your persona? Do you spend time in nature? Are you optimistic, or learning to be? Are you aware of your inner chatterbox? Are you conscious of your fears? Are you in the "now" more? Are you aware of your attachments and addictions such as food, drink, shopping and technology etc.? Do you create? Can you sit quietly in silence just being? Can you be wrong and let it go, even if you are factually right? Can you shut up? Can you speak up? Do you laugh? Do you cry? Is smiling an effort or not? Do you sleep well? Do you judge and evaluate others and situations? Do you make excuses? Do you blame? Do you complain? Do you have original thoughts, no matter how wacky you or others feel they are? Do you follow the herd? Are you independent? Are your loved ones free from your control in every form? And you from theirs? Do you love who you are? Do you forgive yourself and others? Can you relax? Can you be focused and mindful? Do you walk? Do you ride? Do you run? Do you jump? Do you play? Do you dance? Do you make eye contact? Can you love strangers? Can you love yourself?

Can you love animals? Can you love the sick? Can you love the old? Can you love the young? Can you love the different? Can you love the fat? Can you love the thin? Can you love the homeless tramps? Can you love those conflicting with you? Are you helpful? Are you observant? Are you selfless? Are you accepting of what cannot be changed?

This list is just a small sample of where we can make progress in our lives. Once it becomes clear to us how stuck or set in our ways we have become and the conscious decision to progress is made there are literally dozens of avenues daily that can be explored. The process of getting better will result in a life full of success as every moment of progress is a moment of personal triumph. Each day can be filled with precious fulfilling moments, each moment motivating us on to the next.

 **Learning - The Aliveness of Progress**

All we can do, and all we will do is to learn what we are ready to learn. And all that takes is an absorption in learning, in observing, in contemplation and in trying to understand our own nature. This active learning is participatory, is life long and interesting, in its own way it's a joy.

**Education is not the learning of facts, but the training of the mind to think.**

— Albert Einstein

We are in the position of looking around from where we are standing, our starting point and observing those areas we do not understand and that are still unknown. We are all in that position and it provides access to constant freshness and the delight of discovering the new, the unseen and the yet uncontrolled, this is the aliveness of progress.

Don't be scared that we will fail, that we will make mistakes and not guess under which rock the prize is hidden. There is no prize to be found. There is only the process of becoming more balanced, more authentic, and truly alive. If we observe, we will see exactly what our eyes are able to see and use at that precise moment and if we can have some faith in that process, we will enjoy our lives and progress and be free from the fear that imprisons us where we are now.

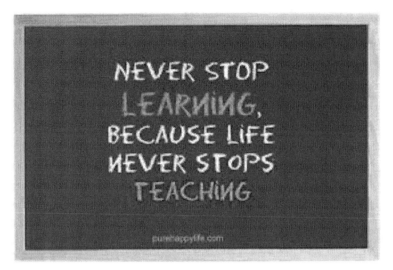

There is nothing to fear, nothing to lose, only the adventure of learning, of release, of curiosity and awe at the expansive reality, exceeding anything we have experienced, yet to which we are as one.

 **Soul2Whole – Life Coaching**

We teach best what we need to learn. Even though I make my living from life coaching, I will discuss it with the firm belief that, throughout life, we are all life coaches and it is only my awareness and specialist work that separates myself from my partners (clients). We can all make a big difference to others in our interactions every day. In my work I fully expect to progress as much, if differently, as my partners in every encounter. Developing every aspect of our psyches and bodies to full potential and to help others progress likewise in a genuine, loving and compassionate way. We are all more the same than different once the fake conditioning has been stripped away.

We are all therapists to ourselves and others. Becoming whole in life requires positive action. Every moment and interaction has the seeds of positive change contained within. Every moment is therapy. Each precious moment with others can result in progress. It will result in change of some kind, as every encounter does, either a little or a lot. It is wise to seek out these difficult encounters as they result in more growth and progress than one could ever achieve sitting on a mountain top retreat.

Human beings have a genetic tendency toward becoming whole, self- realized, self-actualized or whatever term you would prefer to describe human beings getting close to and beyond our accepted potential in all areas of life. It is believed that as sure as an acorn will become an oak tree, human beings will become self-actualized once all obstacles to progress have been removed.

Having said that it then becomes clear that the task of a life coach is to remove obstacles to allow us as individuals to mature and realize our full potential. Our purpose in life becomes to reveal the most complete person we can be. I will call this our Soul-self.

Life coaching is the practice of removing obstacles and motivating progress in every aspect of our individual lives in order to get better and ultimately to reveal our Soul-Selves. To make the inevitable changes that we undergo throughout life the most positive and life affirming possible.

Progress then is more often a process of unlearning all that hides our true potential, by changing habits and the way we think in order to harmonize our lives and flow with life as opposed to resisting our true natures. We have played a variety of roles our entire lives, these roles get in the way of true progress. Progress for the human organism is often not visible unless it is obvious change with our most precious gift, our body or change in our material world. Otherwise, progress is recognized and felt inside subtly as a kind of peaceful knowing and acceptance of being in control and in the flow of life.

What does become more obvious are those times when our ego personas are in charge, the contrast is more obvious and we feel as if we have failed in letting the ego dominate us. As if possessed by a well-meaning stranger. The feeling is one of being taken over and running on frenzied autopilot against our true natures. We become the observers of our over industrious ego personas. No longer convinced by the roles that we play. No longer distracted to the point of not even noticing. These instance are generally in reaction to another ego persona being present and the energies clashing. Often it is our families more likely to engage this side of us. However, each experience is a valuable lesson to take into our next encounter. We become less reactionary and more in control. Eventually people become attracted to our sacred self, in what appears on the outside to be the new you and this you eventually, and with some effort, becomes the dominant self. This is not achieved by hate and aggression for a part of oneself but rather by aligning persona, shadow and soul in an authentic and loving union. The many becomes the one. Our external worlds can change beyond recognition as we attract different people and will probably repel old ego driven friends. Like seems to attract like. As mentioned previously this may entail feeling out of step with a society that is often turbulent, forced and ego driven, due to the ego domination of most members of any society created by the controlling structures put in place for profit and control by the hidden powers that manipulate our worlds. We must lovingly proceed with our progress despite what goes on behind our backs.

Mastering the art of individuality is mastering how to live lovingly in society without becoming an automaton or becoming the product of that society. It entails change and often a changing of the guard in your life to match up to the higher energy of the authentic person that re-emerges. It does not contain resistance of any kind but rather an accepting and merging state of mind. As befitting the goal of the many becoming the one or the fragmented psyche becoming whole.

How do we make progress work in the real world?

In our life coaching practice we are able to affect progress in many areas of life. Exercise, nutrition, relationships, vocation, motivation, addictions & attachments and many other areas in which our partners (clients) are feeling that progress has stopped or in which they are regressing. Just feeling plain stuck in a rut. This must be done without getting lost in the ego behaviors attached to many of our progress areas.

> *"At no point do I claim any special mastery over how to live life, but I am committed to finding a formula through experience that could assure a person some success".*
> - Benjamin Franklin.

I am probably not alone in spending the majority of my life believing myself ordinary and unexceptional and as such with nothing of interest to say to people on how they may live their lives. Retrospectively I have always had this feeling of never really belonging in groups and a feeling of being the odd one out in most group situations. A good example would be on the odd occasion I would go to a soccer match with my friends.  They would comfortably exhibit the herd behaviour seen as normal in that situation I would just feel silly and not understand the behaviour at all, finding it, for want of a better word, senseless.

Thus I would end the experience feeling that there was something wrong with me in that I could not enjoy the bonding as the others so obviously were. In fact, I think the herd had the opposite effect on me and rather than provide a place to hide away or to be comfortable and avoid personal responsibilities, the experience actually made me feel more separate and I felt that all others could see I did not belong and were aware of my discomfort. Rather than hide in the crowd I felt exposed and vulnerable in the crowd. I do now wander just how many of them were authentically in the moment and how many were being inauthentic and just playing their expected roles as football supporter things. However, I have learned how to adapt rather than become comfortable and can "fit in" with the required herd mentality albeit begrudgingly at times, even more so in recent times. I notice the behaviors in others before I notice them in myself but it is a good place to look for where I need to get better. My attitude has changed from one of a kind of apologetic inability to tailor myself to each and every group situation, to an attitude of understanding that it is ok to be just how I am and my freedom is to be found in that, and other choices that previously I had felt separated me from society in a negative way. I think the best way to explain myself is that up to the point that I consider my awakening my life lived me. I was sleepwalking through a life that was based on others, norms and societies expectations. I had little awareness of the situation and believed myself to be freely living my own life. However, the nagging doubts and anxieties were ever present and I forever tried to find peace of mind in more is better. More stuff, more fun, just more distractions in general but those "something missing" moments never really left me. Material gains and hedonistic pleasure were my unfulfilling answers and the short term solutions to my problems. I see now that that is the case for many "normal" members of our society and they are lost in the more is better philosophy in the search for that promised happiness that they believe they deserve and is possible because it has been promised, and is promised every day in many ways. They were the wrong answers. They will never be the right answers. That next new car, holiday, gadget, relationship or night out will do very little but postpone the search for that deeper meaning that we all crave in reality but are for too distracted to ever give any real thought to obtaining

I now live my life as opposed to being carried along by norms and opinions. I dare to be myself and aim for authenticity as much as I can. I am also aware that 100% authenticity may be unattainable as we are conditioned from birth to behave inauthentically.

Be careful when you blindly follow the Masses...
sometimes the 'M' is silent.

**DO YOU SEE 'HERD MENTALITY' AROUND YOU?**

For the first time in my life I feel I am seeing life and particularly life for an individual in society clearly, or more clearly. The challenge and meaning that brings to my life is invigorating and inspires me to enjoy every moment with a renewed vigour. This renewed vigour or passion is not to be seen and exhibited by external actions but a deeper internal feeling, a passion for life and a life full of eureka moments that make you smile inwardly. For the first time in my life a comfortable feeling of having an understanding of what I can and what I can't expect from my life. A feeling of knowing that the meaning of my life is entirely down to my choices. A feeling of understanding that man will never have all of the answers that he so desires and that that desire for clarity is often misplaced, so misplaced that he would rather invent answers and myths than accept that life is absurd and the clarity pursued by man is unattainable. And lastly a realisation that there are no absolute systems, not science, religion or rational thought that will ever provide the answers for each and every individual on this planet despite their rather extravagant claims of having all of the answers we will ever need. If they do not have the answer, then the problem does not exist. It is up to each individual to create the meaning to their lives and to take responsibility. You have more choices than you realise and there are never any guarantees that you will make the right choice or that when a choice doesn't work out that the other choice would have worked out any better. Choose and move on. The way forward is through awareness of what is and was is not and can never be. And an awareness that you as an individual are pure possibilities and you are constantly becoming, constantly renewing yourself till the day you eventually become a fixed entity, the day you expire.

This book is designed to help the reader progress by breaking free of at least some of the society conditioning and automaton thoughts that pervade any culture. Thoughts that are aimed at social control, security and profit for the ruling classes rather than for the good of the individual. I am thinking and attempting to live this philosophy at times against the society grain each and every day. Sometimes I manage to live free and authentically and at other times I get dragged back into the comfort of herd mentality and inauthenticity. The project never ends and the aim is to live a truly free individual life in a society that will assimilate you totally back into the collective with its considered normal and expected beliefs and behaviors if you choose to surrender your freedom. That is the fate that awaits if I relax even for one second. What a buzz that passion creates inside, what a challenge, every day a life to be lived by me or given to relative comfort and conformity.

> *"In every encounter with reality man is already beyond this encounter. He knows about it, he compares it, he is tempted by other possibilities, he anticipates the future as he remembers the past. This is his freedom, and in this freedom the power of his life consists. It is the source of his vitality, of his life power"* - Paul Tillich.

 **The Spirit Of Progress**

I once fell in love with a small yellow car. I thought it was original and unique and I eventually purchased it, it was the last car I ever bought. But that wasn't because it was yellow, that was because I decided that cars were a part of my life that I needed to break free from for a while until such time as I could be sure that any car would enhance my life as opposed to being an attachment, a thing that I had become dependent on and an addictive feeling that I couldn't live without this machine. I had to break the habit in order to progress my life away from the excessive dependency on technology. It really had become a matter of breaking free from this attachment and others that dominate our society in a way that we feel is harmless as it gives us something shiny at the same time as taking our freedom away. The measure has to be – does the technology enhance the human organism (you) or does it in some way make us less human or detract in any way from our reaching our full potential as human beings. Very often the old saying "anything in moderation" works very well but it seems to be human nature and the nature of capitalism to obsessively use and exploit any enhancement until it no longer offers any benefits to our human development and becomes an addiction that we are too happy to accept as the norm.

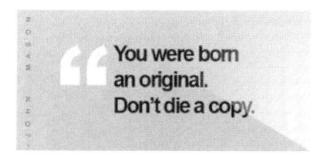

**You were born an original. Don't die a copy.**

So here I am in this small yellow car that is so different from every other car on the road when it suddenly hit me that there are hundreds of the same model and the same colour. Before the purchase they must have been invisible but after the purchase they appeared in my perception constantly. The fact is we shut out any sensory information we deem unnecessary and before the yellow car which I named Sarah, I had no room for yellow cars in my perception but once Sarah had come into my life I could see Sarah's everywhere, as they had always been but shut out from my sensing. I had a similar experience when founding progress therapy, before the event I had not really noticed it but once I included progress in my life, I could see it everywhere, in every situation by either the lack of progress or the progressive nature of a situation.

When I decided to make the spirit of progress my speech for my speaking club's annual contest, I began to see examples of personal progress everywhere. The first being that I, with the personality type of an introverted, intuitive feeler had progressed from thought to action in taking on the challenge of public speaking.

On the evening of the contest we drew lots to decide the order we would speak. I generally prefer to be first so I can relieve my nerves A.S.A.P. I drew last in both the speaking contest and the evaluation contest. It looks as if I may have some work to do on this law of attraction thing, I got the opposite to my expectations twice. Or so I thought at the time. This turned out to be a blessing as the fine speeches that proceeded mine were full of useable examples of how courageous people had chosen to progress their lives when faced with moments when many would have chosen the easier option of regression or conformity to the will of others and popular opinion in what might be considered hopeless situations. Many would have chosen not to rock the society boat. Fortunately, I do not plan my speech in too much detail and could comfortably use this new material in a progressive way.

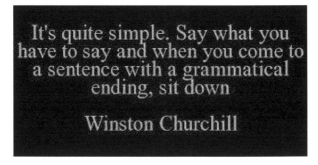

It's quite simple. Say what you have to say and when you come to a sentence with a grammatical ending, sit down

Winston Churchill

"In this seminar we'll discuss a simple technique for overcoming your fear of speaking in public."

The first example was of a young African lady that had followed her dream and married young, only as often happens for that dream to explode in her face. Finding herself unhappy and trapped in an abusive marriage with a partner she now barely recognised from the man she married. Divorce was widely considered against the cultural norms under any circumstances. It was just not the thing to do. This young lady found the courage to free herself and find a happier life. Choosing to progress against the wishes of even her closest loved ones.

The next young man to speak was told he would never amount to anything by one of his teachers and rather than subscribe to his teacher's point of view as an authority figure he used that moment as a springboard to change and progress. Both of these speeches were fine examples of individuals discovering against the odds that there is always another choice for the brave. Choosing the spirit of progress is always an option. There was also a speech aptly named progressive communication, setting the stage perfectly for my "spirit of progress" speech coming up last. It was becoming even clearer to me as I sat and listened that progress is a vital value in the world of humans. And maybe I was not that lucky but progress really is that visible in our lives once we start to notice and choose it for ourselves. I was to find more evidence for this to be the case.

"The human brain starts working the moment you are born and never stops until you stand up to speak in public." ~ Sir George Jessel

My next opportunity to speak was a week later and once again of the four speeches ahead of mine 3 of them were tales of progress and one was a regressive speech about using humour to mask a deep rooted obesity issue. I was able to use the four speeches as examples. It was the first time I had witnessed a regressive speech in my time at toastmasters. However, the speaker was totally unaware of the regressive nature of his speech, rather thinking it was progressive to use jokes to avoid what were obviously some quite serious weight issues. It was not too difficult to look past the humour within this speech and draw some quite serious conclusions as to the state of mind of the speaker. Another example of the complexity of the human psyche. We are indeed complex organisms.

My speech was to be evaluated. This means that four speakers would each speak for three minutes about my speech. Praise, constructive criticism and recommendations. Basically they were to rip the shit out of it and I was to sit and smile. I love a test and I really did have only the merest hint of ego in this moment which is on itself a major breakthrough for me as I once would have hated any criticism at all having been raised by a family that did little else bit criticise and s still do. On the whole I received an amazing response, the criticism and recommendations were constructive or stuff that I was aware of already.

I actually volunteered to be the target speaker as I feel that it is not possible for any of us to progress unless we take on board knowledge of any possible barriers or obstacles to our progress highlighted by well-meaning others. We need to be in the firing line in order to become bullet proof. This way we can continue on to towards reaching our potential. We do have to deal with criticism from those not so well-meaning but we can develop an intuition for knowing and then smiling and ignoring those people. Hopefully they will catch up some time. Letting go of such moments with a shrug is a vital life skill.

Reaching a potential that is as yet unknown, we can only guess as to what may be our limits often based on the past. I hesitate to use the word limitless because human potential may have limits but at this point in time there is no sign of any such limits apart from those self-imposed or conditioned into us from birth and by others every day. These can all be transcended. It is our purpose in life to transcend any previously perceived limitations and further the mind boggling progress of our species starting with ourselves. We are generally so limited by our conditioned beliefs that we are virtually living life in a straight jacket.

It is widely argued that we have a tendency as humans to self-actualise or as I prefer to say to become more whole. The theory follows that it is a matter of removing barriers and obstacles to progress and allowing the process to naturally unfold in each unique individual. We put many of the barriers in place ourselves encouraged by our rulers, capitalists and the media through fear and in order that we are able to navigate our way through the maze of society in our fledgling years, which can last until midlife or for many the entirety of our lives.  What follows are some thoughts and ideas on how we can foster and live our lives in an all pervasive spirit of progress for the good of ourselves, others and ultimately all of life on this earth.

The whole Toastmasters adventure is part of my journey of progressing to wholeness by progressing bit by bit in every aspect of my life. This is easy in the stuff that I would consider my strengths but working on my perceived weaknesses is whole different ball game. I am not a toastmaster forever or anything like that but the experience like all experiences has enabled me to develop in areas that I deemed I needed to work on.

What follows is the written version of the speech that I had only seven minutes to deliver. I hope it begins to create a spirit of progress in you that will expand and grow as you become more whole. This book is filled with help and advice to help you progress. You will start to see opportunities for progress everywhere once you begin to live your life in the spirit of progress.

**P**ASSIONATE POTENTIAL

**R**ELAXED RECONNECTION

**O**PEN MINDED OPTIMISM

**G**RATEFUL GENEROSITY

**R**EGRESSION

**E**DUCATED IGNORANCE

**S**ILENT SURRENDER

**S**ERVICE WITH SPARKLE

### Passionate Potential

We can never progress towards our individual potential unless we are both passionate and free. In actual fact we can never be classed as individuals unless we are free. We may not be as free as we believe ourselves to be.

Philosopher Soren Kierkegaard argues that passion is not outside of

"A man who as a physical being is always turned toward the outside, thinking that his happiness lies outside him, finally turns inward and discovers that the source is within him."

**Soren Kierkegaard**

us, it centres on a kind of focus and intensity, a type of deliberateness about how we go about things. He calls it inwardness. Passionate people are inward because they strive to exist as individual subjects and not as labelled objects.

A labelled abject has no choice about how to exist, it does what the world dictates and expects it to do, it conforms. Stereotyping attempts, with much success, to turn a subject into an object, into a thing. Subjects decide for themselves how to be in the world.

A life full of passion is full of engagement and a life of engaged passion emphasises how you go about living and not what you end up doing. In order to be free and passionate about life we need to be "true to ourselves". Living passionately involves being free subjects as opposed to captive objects. I will discuss freedom and subjectivity now, plucked from my university dissertation briefly covering the subjects.

Passionate potential can only be achieved by free subjects.

MAN IS

# CONDEMNED TO BE FREE;

BECAUSE ONCE

## THROWN INTO THE WORLD,

HE IS

# RESPONSIBLE

FOR

## EVERYTHING HE DOES.

SARTRE

**Freedom** - Sartre claims our immersion in physical, historical and social structures does not undermine our freedom. We inherit these structures and the way they act on us is out of our control. They can be seen as a limiting situation but it is in these situations that we are motivated to act.  These structures cannot by themselves deprive us of our freedom.  Sartre refers to everything you can't control as your facticity, your native nationality, whether you were born rich or poor, the political circumstances you live in - these factors are all out of your immediate control.  Furthermore, Sartre argues that freedom is essentially connected to negativity.  Any action is on principle intentional and done so with purpose. The first negative is rejecting what is the current state of affairs.  The second negative is the aim to bring about a state of affairs that is currently not.  This is common to all genuine actions.  You are free when you have a choice.  You choose how to interpret your situation.  You choose how to react to your situation and finally you choose whether to remain in your situation.  Sartre stresses what he calls being-for others.  This is when you are reduced to an object in the world of others. In order to regain freedom one must reject the current state of affairs and create a state of affairs that has yet to exist.

Foucault's theory on freedom is not being in answer to the question, "Are we free?" but instead in answer to the question, "How are we historically restrained and what can we do about it?"

These constraints do not operate by stopping people from doing what they want.  Instead they create people to be and behave in certain kinds of ways, thus making them into docile bodies. Furthermore, theory states that power according to Foucault makes us certain types of people.  It trains our bodies to behave in certain ways and it makes us think of ourselves in certain ways.  This constraint works to limit individual options, it creates a conformity and minimises the possibilities of resistance or experimentation with other forms of living.

By the same token if we understand our historical legacy and the power and forces at work there is no reason we cannot change it that is freedom. If we understand our situation, then we have a chance at changing it. Foucault describes how alternative ways of living are constrained by who we are made to be and how we think of ourselves.

Capturing the idea that freedom is not simply a matter of being left to ourselves but also a matter of reinventing ourselves into what we would like to be. What's more for Foucault freedom is a matter of experimentation, to try out different possible transformations to see where they may lead.

> *"We are, then, neither helpless in the face of what moulds us nor certain of what we can do about it. We are somewhere in-between. That is where our freedom lies, and indeed that is what our freedom is............ Freedom is not the same as liberation. Whether our freedom is liberating or not is something that is not guaranteed to us"* - Foucault.

To experiment with alternate ways of living and finding freedom, passion would be an essential ingredient to success.

**Subjectivity** - Foucault's theory and practice of subjectivity argues that with all the pressures and impulses to conform, we mask and deny ourselves, one's true self is often lost (lost soul). We say what others want us to say and act the way we are expected by others to act and in the process we lie to ourselves, betray ourselves, forget ourselves, let ourselves down and neglect ourselves. And yet amongst all of these obstacles we still seek out the true authentic self and life. Facing the task of being ourselves is what Foucault calls the care for the self. He defines our subjectivity as what we make ourselves when we devote ourselves to taking care of ourselves. Adding that we find ourselves constantly seeking the approval of others for a value and recognition that becomes very important to us. The need for real self-examination becomes less intense with the realisation that life, as it turns out, has been laid out before us. Daily nudging, encouraged, instructed and firmly pushing in the proper direction. It is easy enough to absorb much of what it needs to be known to survive in the world, to follow the path robot-like.

"This ready-made character of life comes from interacting with experts and authorities who are there to help me become a well-adjusted, happy, healthy productive member of society......central to this is the way it focuses attention on me, you and everyone else as an object of both control and knowledge...not governed in a way that represses or oppresses but in a way that feels best for me" - Foucault

Furthermore' it is in this disciplinary context that we often decide to look for a true self that rebels against the moulding and discipline of governmentality and escape from the disciplined self. Moreover, becoming oneself is a strenuous action. Foucault looks at this and makes much of it being a work of art, a creation of self, and an exercise by which the true self establishes a relationship of distance from the disciplined self. When we become fixed our actions become meaningless, no matter what we do, we are still the fixed person we have conceived for ourselves. The true self is never fixed, and is a continuous becoming, an art of no longer being what I was and experimenting towards unknown futures.

It can be thought that subjectivity is a state that we occupy. For Foucault subjectivity is an activity we perform which always takes place in a field of constraint, he calls these activities practices of the self and they may include writing, diet and exercise.  Note that the practises are all areas that we would hope to progress in.

The constraint comes from the more general prevailing norms and values of the society of which we are a part.

Progress can only be achieved by first being aware and then mastering the art of individuality.

Mastering The Art of Individuality.

Sartre refers to everything you can't control as your facticity, your native nationality, whether you were born rich or poor, the political circumstances you live in - these factors are all out of your immediate control.  Furthermore' Sartre claims our immersion in physical, historical and social structures does not undermine our freedom.  Now this discussion will look at what action an individual can take to determine themselves and also how a coherent sense of self can be reclaimed and developed through awareness of being objectified and labelled.

Should you uncritically accept certain ways of seeing things you are engaging with the world in ways created by others?  Are you willing to call this perspective an expression of what you are as a unique individual?  The first point would be that you would have to be interested in attributing meaning to your life otherwise you would be quite happy accepting the meaning given to your life by others. This acceptance of yourself as an object created by others is what existentialists would term an inauthentic way to live and rejection of your freedom to choose your life's meaning.

Similarly, Foucault's theory and practice of subjectivity argues that with all the pressures and impulses to conform, to mask and deny ourselves, one's true self is often lost.  We say what others want us to say and act the way we are expected by others to act and in the process we lie to ourselves, betray ourselves, forget ourselves, let ourselves down and neglect ourselves.

Having become interested in a search for meaning in your life, you can then turn to appreciating that living as an individual requires that you engage with the world in a way that expresses your uniqueness.  Living self critically to control elements of your life that aren't reflective of you and being honest about the self at all times to avoid self-deceptions.

Are there any practical tools that can be considered?

Foucault's concept of critique suggests some positive steps that an individual may take towards retaining individuality.

Foucault's notion of critique which emerges from and is linked to governmentality techniques. Foucault conceptualises critique as the art of not being governed quite so much and the art of navigating power relations.  Critique retains a critically self-reflexive character and therefore possesses the potential to emancipate the agent from being determined by the relations of power.  Leaving the capacity to take up norms differently or not at all solely to the individual. Foucault does supply tools to facilitate insubordinate constitution of ourselves.  The values he thought a critical attitude can be cultivated with if chosen and practiced are as follows:

**Refusal** - refusing to accept as self-evident the things that are proposed to us.

**Curiosity** - the need to analyse and to know since we can accomplish nothing without reflection and knowledge.

I HAVE NO SPECIAL TALENTS. I AM ONLY PASSIONATELY CURIOUS.

-ALBERT EINSTEIN

**Innovation** - to seek out in our reflection those things that have never been thought or imagined.

Furthermore, Foucault stated that he engaged in and endeavoured to promote these values in his philosophical work.  As can be appreciated this process requires constant action and will not just happen.

It can be seen here that although one may be to some degree determined by facticity - physical, historical and social structures that this in no way undermines your freedom to create and interpret your unique sense of self and give meaning to who you are.

### Relaxed Reconnection

Once we have become aware of the constraints our lives operate under and where our freedom to progress can be found we can move on to progressing within those constraints through the wonderful life opportunities that allow us to become whole.

Reconnection is one such avenue to be explored. Living in our high tech world it is a fact of life that in the first part of life we are so focused on finding a position of safety, security and status within the world that we totally lose touch with Gaia – the earth viewed as a vast self-regulating organism – in doing so we neglect to take care of our souls. I will share a short anecdote with you now to show how this became obvious in my world.

It's happening in this moment

Birds, what birds? - I got to pondering whilst out walking the other day how at one time during my head up my arse years, I remember vividly believing that all of the birds were vanishing from the planet. This belief was based on birds being very much a part of my experience when I was growing up as a child and young man but seeming to disappear as the years passed by. However, some years ago as I made a conscious effort to become more human again and I am reconnecting to nature, I once again have become aware of the birds and wildlife all around us. Nowadays, I have many precious moments thanks to Mother Nature.

My conclusion is that I had become so distracted with living my life in a distracted society that I had disconnected myself from nature. I had become unconscious when it came to noticing anything that wasn't geared to my amassing a bigger pile of stuff and achieving the success I needed to impress others.

The birds were here all along I had just stopped noticing them. A state that I believe is a society affliction that needs to be cured. I wonder what else we become unconscious of when we are distracted in building our little empires in the first half of our lives. I honestly believe that connection is the key, or one of the keys to the peace of mind and serenity that so many of us are searching for. Nature is still here and we are part of it.

Getting out and rediscovering what we are part of may actually help with our peace of mind and in the process help us in finding our sacred selves. All of this can be achieved whilst finding success in the material world. It is not a case of either or, we can have both. There is a certain balance to be sought in a life which can be realistically considered successful. Riches are not all about money and stuff. Some of life's more precious moments are just about being present in the moment to be in awe of the world around us.

We are rarely even aware of our isolation from the planet as the considered "normal" behaviour that systematically separates us from our humanity, producing hollow people. Soul-less Human beings, halfway to becoming the technology we worship with such fervour as our modern false idols.

The human tendency to self-actualise, to become whole eventually demands more than a life full of stuff and gadgets and the desire to reconnect becomes a priority in our lives. Often the call is missed and the desire mistaken for a need to amass yet more stuff and search for more hedonistic pleasure the next one hopefully being the one that finally makes us happy. The call having been missed and the stuff and hedonism not delivering the peace of mind expected, the cycle goes on. This for many is how life is from birth until death, an endless cycle of hollow suffering continues as our souls remain uncared for. If we are lucky and just a little bit smarter than average, we decide to search elsewhere for some peace of mind and peace of heart. But sadly it can be readily witnessed that many spend their whole lives with all of their material needs fulfilled but still suffering in their distracted and disconnected lives.

There is an authentic self buried deep in our psyches (soul) that is perfectly connected to Gaia and beyond. That self has been inadvertently buried under erroneous conditioning, distractions and beliefs. Reconnection is the removal of all obstacles and barriers that bar the way to the natural process of becoming whole. An allowing of our fragmented psyche (soul) to align naturally in what has become a very complicated and unnatural world.

71

A good place to start to reconnect is in nature – spending quality time sensing all things in nature. The key is to be present in the moment. Seeing, hearing, feeling, smelling and touching – taking time to notice. No technology. Leave your inner chatterbox at home or at least work to shut it up as much as possible. It gets easier the more you do it. If you talk too much with company, then go alone. This is about our relationship with nature not an opportunity to gossip or put the world to rights.

Finding places to sit and look or close your eyes and listen or feel the breeze caressing your skin or the warmth of the sun on your flesh. Just being present with nowhere to rush off to and no past moments to stress over. This is a precious moment between you and nature. Feel it – value it. I try to be outside with nature at dawn and through sunrise for the whole year. It is worth the early mornings and I have many up close and personal moments with nature because I am there. There is much peace to be found at this time and a thriving natural world abused and neglected by man that still manages to inspire awe and wonder. I have used a picture of a Barn owl with this article as I spend many happy mornings sitting on a log watching them hunting. There were many other possibilities for the starring role. This is on the outskirts of a busy industrial town. Nature is with us, we just have to be present.

We live on a beautiful planet and we don't have to travel far to find nature adapting wonderfully to man's enforced changes and surviving despite our often selfish and mostly inconsiderate presence on this planet.

I would urge anyone to find their regular place for communing with nature year round and soak up the riches that such precious moments bestow on any and all lucky enough to be present. The best moments in life are still free. Relaxed reconnection is caring for your soul by living in the spirit of progress.

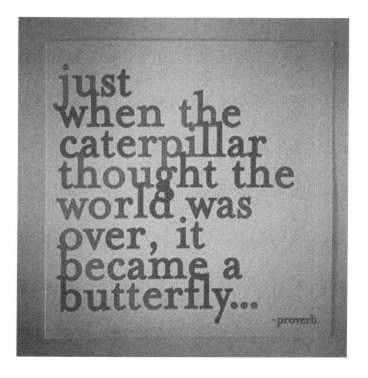

 **Open-Minded Optimism**

We all like the thought that we are open minded but sadly open mindedness is in short supply in the 21st century. The moment we make thoughts and ideas "our" opinions we immediately narrow our minds. The second we join institutions such as political or religious groups we take on their ideas and dogmas as our own and the moment a thing becomes "mine" it becomes attached to one's identity and takes on an inflexibility and power that no thought should ever have. It is better to have thoughts and ideas one likes at this moment but to remain open to the inevitable change in the discovery of progressive thinking and the changes we undergo as individuals and as a collective. We all perceive and process the world in uniquely different ways and progress is the result of that process and the process of life. Ever changing in every moment. "This to will pass" is applicable to each moment of pleasure and pain.

Stubbornly holding on to ideas and beliefs stunts personal progress which inevitably stunts the growth of cultures. Narrow (closed) mindedness has always been the root cause of unrest and hostility in societies. Resistance to change halts progress in many areas. Science and religion being the most obvious narrow minded culprits.

Please remember at this point I am not discussing material progress which in no way indicates a progressive humanity. It could be argued that material progress has quite the opposite effect. Making for cultures in which the seven deadly sins of lust, gluttony, greed, sloth, anger, envy and pride have become admired traits for the up and coming young human, hungry for material progress.

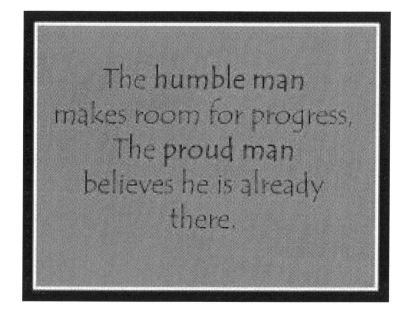

The humble man
makes room for progress,
The proud man
believes he is already
there.

It is vitally important when dealing with new ideas and thoughts that we listen openly no matter how resistant we feel or how conditioned we are to our existing thoughts. Allowing time and further investigation through curiosity and detaching ourselves from the thoughts as part of our identity is the way to remain open to progress no matter how illogical ideas may seem upon first exposure.

Change is inevitable and the choice must be for personal progress. Open mindedness encourages progress. Narrow minded resistance is regressive. Wisdom gained through knowledge, experience and intuition are the tools at our disposal for making progress choices. Open mindedness fosters the spirit of progress.

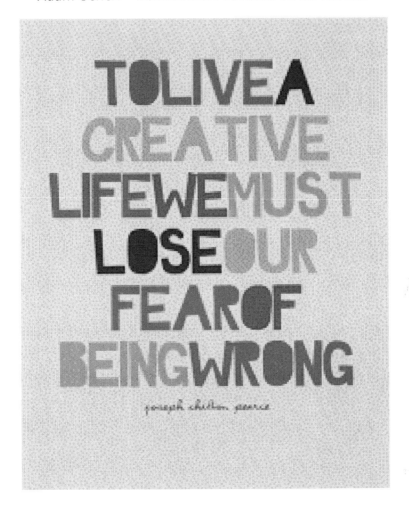

TO LIVE A CREATIVE LIFE WE MUST LOSE OUR FEAR OF BEING WRONG

joseph chilton pearce

With an open mind optimism for the possibilities in every situation becomes real. It was once believed that we are fixed as either optimistic, pessimistic or somewhere in-between. However, it is now known that we can learn to be optimistic cognitively. Martin Seligman's book Learned Optimism shows how through questioning our thoughts and beliefs rationally we can turn negative pessimistic beliefs on their heads in a way that makes us more optimistic and better able to deal with life's inconveniences that were once thought as catastrophes.

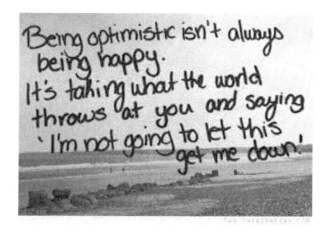

Surrounding yourself with optimistic people will help also and distancing yourself from pessimists at least until you are able through your new learned optimism not to let them affect you is also a wise move. Removing obstacles to your progress is what your journey is based on and this includes toxic people until you are so strong that it is you that affects them with your open minded optimism. You will feel inside of yourself when you are ready and when you need to beat a hasty retreat in lower energy situations. This last sentence will make sense at the right time for you.

An open minded optimistic attitude makes progress inevitable and more importantly creates great expectations for our lives. You will see that as we progress through the pages of this book the spirit we are creating is one that will almost guarantee some success.

 **Grateful Generosity**

It is a trap we all fall into to take the good in our lives for granted or interpret it as bad and rather than be grateful show ingratitude due to our greed and envy of what others have more than us. Endlessly complaining about the weather and wanting more stuff in our lives. Believing that sunshine and a big pile of stuff will finally bring us the happiness we somehow feel we deserve and the peace of mind we so crave that will never come until we accept being human comes with a level of anxiety built in with the gift of consciousness.

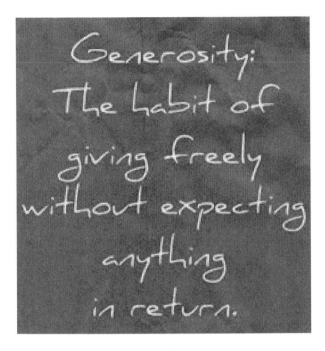

The fact is that resisting and wanting are two major contributors to the unhappiness, anxiety and that restlessness we feel will disappear when and if only! Accepting a level of anxiety, eliminating resistance and being satisfied with what you have and not wanting what you don't have is the solution to that little problem.

As with any progress we contain the solutions inside of ourselves. It is easy for me to suggest that we gratefully accept our lives and recognise the precious moments or that we should count our blessings, both are true but what exactly does that mean and how might it work in reality?

When our responses to life are conditioned and mostly negative our task is to re-program our on board computer (brain) to a more positive state of mind at a deep level. Responses to external events that bring on conditioned negative reactions and feelings as the norm need to be changed. New habits are what is needed.

To re-wire my brain and to facilitate the changes in my life I have days of focus at which time I dedicate a whole day to developing new habits and responses that are more fitting to my personal progress and that become the norm for me. One such day is "Choose Tuesday".

"I Choose Tuesday" is dedicated to spending the day consciously choosing how I wish to react and feel. I begin early in my reflective time. I choose safety and security, peace, love, Julie, serenity, to choose, the pups (my dogs), the plant gang (all named individually), accepting what is, honesty and so on. I have a list of over 100 values and ad lib according to my moods and situations that develop. To choose for me is to be grateful. When I walk I choose wind, rain, mud and all of nature. Choosing melts away resistance and teaches that to flow with what is happening leads to greater peace of heart and mind than resisting a world that we can't change. I will discuss choosing in greater length later in the book.

I call this new habit and new learned responses a soul shrug. Once noise and turbulence in our lives is no longer resisted is fades away from our reality. Just soul shrug and let it go. Choosing and being grateful is a much more peaceful state of mind from which to view life.

If we can't deal with the weather without having a mental breakdown, what chance have we when a serious problem comes along?

Change from the inside leads to many more precious moments in situations which normally are resisted and as a consequence they persist day after day. Being more in step in the dance of life creates a more harmonious reality with nature and with others. Nobody said it will be easy but it is worth it.

Nothing is excluded from this gratitude attitude and the resulting generosity it creates. Inside of ourselves, wanting to give something back becomes more than an annoying cliché uttered by egos trying to fool themselves and others, it becomes an automatic behaviour that is not even talked about. Gratitude and generosity become habits and not values to bolster ego status by looking good for others.

When we feel that life is giving to us constantly it is the most natural thing in the world that we would want to reciprocate and once we realise that giving feels so amazing another new habit is formed. The path of gratitude coincides with the path of generosity.

By choosing my reality and accepting my lessons every "Choose Tuesday" my grateful state of mind expands across the whole of my week. This is the spirit of progress. I react in a more life affirming way to testing situations, extracting the lessons in order to progress. Once more a spirit of optimism pervades my life. The soul shrug is a very useful tool and the motion is like releasing a pressure valve. Resistance leaves the body as your whole self shrugs in acceptance.

Are we ignoring and repressing our darker sides?

The next section shows how our greatest lessons will come from our darkest moments and that aligning with all that we are is the only road to wholeness.

 **Regression**

It is important to understand that progress is never a straight line to our goals or to improvement in general. In every value there is the opposite contained, in this case the opposite of progression is regression.

How we react to moments or periods of regression may well be the determining factor as to whether we eventually progress according to our great expectations. The most important point is to accept these periods as part of our progress if we can't affect them by our actions. Just shrug and move on maintaining our progressive spirit, one cannot exist without the other. The path of progressing towards any goal or planned outcome is always zigzag. Constantly re-aligning to get back on course. Maintaining a progressive state of mind in spite of perceived adversity is crucial to progressing towards wholeness. Seeing the opportunity in the regressive moments is the art to progress.

Asking yourself "what is the lesson for me here in this moment?"

The greatest lessons and the periods of much progress are to be found in the darkest moments of adversity. Embrace these lessons with gratitude and progress a wiser person. Looking back from a future position of progress you may wish for more dark moments to hasten your development. The regressive periods are often interpreted in hindsight as the defining moments leading to drastic actions and progress. I know this is true for me personally. So much so that I would not change any moment of my life for fear of losing the progressive lessons contained in those dark nights of the soul.

Learning to cherish as part of life the periods of depression, anxiety and despair with minimal resistance has been the way to some peace of mind for me. Acceptance of these states as all being an integral part of the human condition shuts off the resistance or at least lessens the resistance and the flow always returns eventually. Learning to know oneself is a task for life. This also is in the spirit of progress. This attitude is skilful use of the mind.

## Educated Ignorance

On the continuing road progressing towards self-actualisation it is easy to follow our conditioning and believe we are either one half of an opposite or the other – masculine or feminine, proud or humble, good or bad. If we are to continue to progress, then we must understand that we contain everything. All opposites are contained within us. It is alignment rather than picking one over the other that is crucial to our development. All else leads to repression and ultimately problems due to that repression.

A good example is the balance of education and ignorance, no matter what we are led to believe we are not either or but rather a delicate balance of both. It was a truly wise man (Socrates) who admitted at the oracle in Delphi that he knew nothing and from that day became known as the wisest man alive.

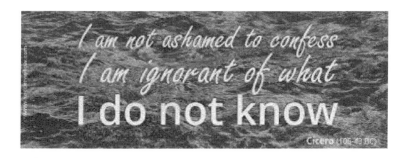

In answer to the question of which of any pair of opposites describes what we are, the answer is always both. If that is not the answer, then that must be the goal to attain balance and wholeness. For Socrates revelation he was proclaimed the wisest of men, a title that still holds for him today, but maybe only amongst other such humble original thinkers.

Socrates state of mind ensured his mind was kept wide open for further knowing, progress, knowledge, experiences and ultimately wisdom. We can never know everything, the wonders of life, death and everything in-between and beyond will endlessly unfold before us in every moment. Infinitely enriching our lives and all that living those lives entails. There are lessons constantly and an educated ignorance keeps us perfectly in the spirit of progress.

 **Silent Surrender**

Silent surrender is an attitude of accepting the feeling of resistance in any situation and shrugging and letting that resistance go. For example, when involved in a conversation where we are feeling that what we want to say is the most important thing in the world and we need the other person to shut up or we are interrupting them. This is a resistant moment that needs us to smile, shrug and realise the relative unimportance of the moment compared to the consequences of continuing the resistance.

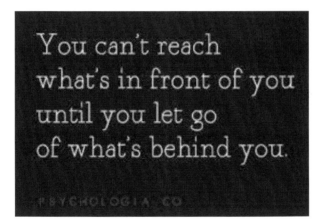

We feel silent surrender instantly, it is a kindness to ourselves and others. These moments do occur for all of us regularly throughout the day. The moment when our ego wants conflict to show how much better we are than others, this is the moment when the soul-shrug works for us. As we feel the blood boiling we just shrug and release the pressure instantly. The more we soul-shrug the better we get at releasing these moments and being kind to ourselves and others.

 ## Service With Sparkle

Many years ago during my silly years, a good friend once warned me of a relationship issue I was having by pointing out that my partner may give their sparkle to someone else and I would lose it. I discovered in hindsight that this was her way of letting me know she could see it happening. A warning without betraying either my partner or myself from a good friend caught in the crossfire.

The concept of us having a sparkle to share with others has stayed with me all these years and I have come to know the sparkle as a reality that humans exude when relating to others with love. The goal would be to sparkle for every encounter in and with life.

When first hearing about the concept for happiness of living a life serving others with purpose, I, of course like everybody else picked up litter, volunteered and looked for good deeds to serve. All of this is very worthy but mostly external deeds and not automatically done in the right spirit. I came across many others that did not enjoy their serving and saw it as more of a duty from which they couldn't escape. And to be totally honest there was not enough voluntary work to serve the do gooders. I was fed up with the line "I wanted to make a difference" that seemed to be uttered parrot fashion by most of the volunteers. I felt the need to strangle the next person that wanted to make a difference. That was hardly in the spirit of kindness but I just felt the whole situation was fake for many of the volunteers. Possibly including myself in that group. It seemed for many an effort to be civil to the person next to them. For young people it was something to put on a resume. I was perplexed at this situation. A whole host of useful, worthy if dishonest volunteers with the intent of being better than other humans. I guess the "good" was done whether it was with the right intentions or not but it still seemed a little ironic that the motivation was largely selfish and the spirit was not one of kindness and compassion but rather one of duty. We are all works in progress. Then one day it hit me after contemplating for months on how one could do good if there was no longer any doing good vacancies in the town. The town was just too full of good people for any new people to be in service to others. How could I fail to be in service to others just because there were no others to be serviced? It was not a great excuse; I could not be in service to others because the others to be served were all taken. The town was too good already. And yet the general feel of the town was still one of turbulence and hostility. Why was it that people everywhere wanted to do good but that never obviously translated to the town or society as a whole in the day to day business of living together? I even witnessed racism and judgement in groups of volunteers. How was it possible to separate the good acts from the normal behaviour witnessed by us all daily that is anything but good? We are so complicated.

This is what I discovered. We are all others and can all be in service to each other all of the time in every moment. In fact, I decided for myself that true service doesn't need a special group or invitation to materialise as it is a state of mind. It is a way of being that leads to behaving just right in every precious moment that presents to each of us.

The way we are in every moment in every situation and every encounter and thought and idea is how we serve others. A smile, a kind word, deed, thought or simply accepting others as they are and equal is all that we need to progress in harmony with others and indeed, all of life as in Gaia, the entire planet as one whole living organism excluding nothing or no one.

Be the person that makes others feel *special.* Be known for your *kindness* and *grace.*

Whilst all of the other altruistic endeavours are worthy and should be included in any service to others plan it is how we are in every moment that creates a spirit of serving with right thinking and right actions.

How can we improve on that? By adding our own unique sparkle (courtesy of my long missed friend), to each and every encounter. She will never know the legacy she has left for me. "The Sparkle."

When thinking of serving others there is another "E" that is relevant here – Egalitarian.

All people (extend to all life) deserve equal rights and opportunities. In every interaction there are learning opportunities for those involved. The wisdom is gained through the progress made according to the permanent connection we have with others.

Domination or attempting to hold or maintain a superior position over others is regressive for ourselves and our relations with others. Partnerships, where all parties' progress via their unique values and talents being shared with loving gratitude is the way to progress. We all have much to learn from even the most difficult of communications that will allow progress towards wholeness.

It could be argued that the more difficult and testing the situation the more opportunities for learning and progress are contained within that awkward situation.

An egalitarian attitude keeps the mind open for progress.

From this little exercise I know I have a lot of work to do on both knowing myself and getting better. But the beauty of having progress and getting better as a life purpose is that we can all start where we are and move forward. Progress motivates and the rewards are personal and expanding for the soul. Just as the opposite diminishes us. One instinctively knows when something feels right.

**Beauty** – in the eye (mind) of the beholder

Growing up, the title of this piece has meant that we all have different tastes. But do we really or are we conditioned to see beauty as an ideal and very much the same as one another? Often used when we are judging unkindly the beauty of somebody else's partner, car or house or anything we judge as not beautiful via our limited perceptions or through our jealous minds. We may even consider it the opposite, ugly to our own conditioned tastes. Which to all intents and purposes are not even our own but handed to us as being factual and we erroneously believe we have certain tastes regardless of price, brand or any outside influence led by what others may think.

I think we may have missed the full wisdom of this enduring sentence. "Beauty is in the eye of the beholder." Let me explain.

I believe there is a signpost here that will guide us to better understand how all powerful our minds are in our lives. An understanding that will allow us to explore our full human potential. A potential that we tend to take for granted or totally ignore. A full understanding can lead to limitless positive repercussions and subsequent actions that the understanding can deliver to us. A Eureka moment.

The following excerpt is from my daily journal, quickly scribbled some time ago. Upon re-reading it has prompted me to write with this thought about beauty as we know it in black and white for each of us when as usual there are only ever shades of grey. I was having a particularly bad day, which is often the case when the most insightful observations arise.

*"I am spiky today – A little glass half empty, but I see it and I will learn from it. It is quite amazing how from this (half empty) perspective, how my world contains less beauty in all areas than it did previously when it is the same life that I have chosen. I know that just yesterday in my view and it is the same most days to be fair that my life was filled with beautiful sights, sounds and smells. And today that has all changed. What has changed? This just goes to prove to me that my mind and state of mind is what creates the life that I experience. It all starts and finishes with my thoughts, heart and mind. - Life is lived inside out – I am grateful for the beauty in my life even though I am having great difficulty seeing that beauty on this day and this insight to knowing it is in the mind of the beholder through the eyes where beauty is to be found. We create our own beauty but sadly we accept the socially constructed ideals just the same way that we allow ourselves to be conditioned in all aspects of our lives until now. Until we become aware of what is going on behind our backs. Until moments like this that wake us from our slumber."*

On this day I didn't like my music or my home. My dogs were a nuisance and smelly. I didn't want the food I had shopped for. I hated my body, clothes etc. All of which I had chosen and loved.

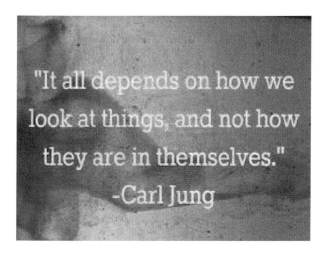

"It all depends on how we look at things, and not how they are in themselves."
-Carl Jung

Our normal reaction in this state is to change our external world in search of something we may find suitably beautiful for our worlds right now. One can see why we are brainwashed into certain ideals of beauty as it narrows our vision and perception of beauty and keeps us buying and scrambling to attain such ideals. Even down to the now infamous trophy wife. What an insult. This is why we spend so much of our hard earned money on all kinds of stuff which we feel will make us happy and our lives more beautiful when in actual fact all we need to do is change our minds and appreciate the beauty that we have in our lives all of the time. We must stop allowing ourselves to be hypnotised by our oppressors so they may control us and take our money. Keeping us chasing an impossible illusory future. On the downside we are and are still being hopelessly brainwashed (for control and to keep the economy healthy) as to what is ideal by greedy and controlling ruling classes and all involved in what is an oppressive regime that we are so used to that we take it as normal and to us it is the norm. The realisation is that it not going to change in a hurry and that to be free we each have to find our own ways to set ourselves free from a collective mentality that enslaves (even those in the thick of it are stuck) and realise the potential we each possess as individuals.

Now to the plus side and there is always a big plus side to being human. We have a choice, we can work to change our minds and regain a priceless ability. The ability to create our lives with our own chosen thoughts. The ability to make our lives beautiful. We can begin by seeing the beauty in all weather conditions to hone our skills. And begin noticing as we watch the television or listen to any media how we are fed suggestions which become our beliefs. Try replacing them with a few of your own and why not defend yourself by turning the crap off.

Using such techniques as affirmations repetitively combined with creative visualisations we can put the beauty back in our lives from the inside out. I began some time ago and the feeling is liberating. Join me in what we, as human beings are capable of and end the seemingly endless exploitation of these same incredible talents by the greedy, controlling tyrant rulers that we have been foolish enough to trust to have our best interests at heart.

Your mind has everything you will ever need. Take back control of yours.

Any day I struggle to find music I like in my massive collection I know it is time to change my mind back to appreciating the beauty in my life. This acts as an early warning system for me. There is a saying for creating peace of mind away from constantly wanting the next thing to make us happy – "Want what you have – Don't want what you don't have."

By using auto-suggestion we can quickly appreciate and become fulfilled with the lives we have created and continue to create through our thoughts and perceptions. Releasing all self-doubt and negativity. Create a beautiful life for yourself as it is a choice you can make, it seems foolish to choose otherwise unless you are a masochist. The sky is not the limit – the mind is and it all starts from here with a single thought.

> *We are governed, our minds are moulded, our tastes formed, our ideas suggested largely by men we have never heard of.*
>
> Edward Bernays

 **Home Sweet Home**

All too often these days our homes have become as they are purely for how they appear to others. And our home is where we go to distract ourselves from life and death. Probably both apply to all of us at some time or another.

For our malevolent rulers our homes have become places where they can enter and brainwash us into feeling abandoned and overwhelmed through the many avenues they now control to infiltrate our most private moments and to cap it all they make us pay for the privilege. Orwellian theories have nothing on the subtle enslavement that we now undergo. It is all packaged so we want it and pay for it. How long before we are clamouring to be chipped as the next big thing? It doesn't take much insight to realise that our every move is choreographed more or less in some devious way or another. They know what we think and do and when we think and do it and who we think and do it with. They also know the how, where and why. But it is all for our own good in the fight against terrorism. Bollox, the only fight we have is with being enslaved by our governments. They are playing us, even in our own homes.

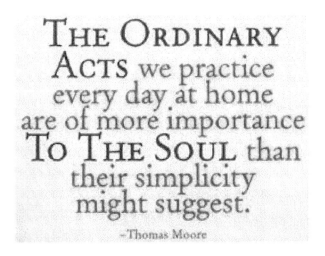

THE ORDINARY ACTS we practice every day at home are of more importance TO THE SOUL than their simplicity might suggest.
-Thomas Moore

Can we at least go some way to taking back our homes from others and our rulers and once again make our homes the place where we reign supreme. A home where we enter diminished from the turbulence of life but are able to emerge re-generated and large into the world once more.

This is only possible if we custom our homes to enhance our unique personalities and break free of many current attachments and addictions that we have been duped to accept as good when in reality they are controlling mechanisms aimed at keeping us docile and predictable. Treating us as little more than organic automatons.

How difficult would it be to guess which addictions, attachments and dependant behaviours are occurring in each home most evenings? None of which could be argued to replenish our souls, let alone afford us the progress and personal growth needed to transform us in each moment so that we may transcend and evolve as individuals and human beings. It is one of my thoughts that our purpose in life is to transcend what it means to be human with each passing generation, simply to get better at being human and to unearth what that really means underneath all of the layers of distraction and false personalities. But make no mistake there are forces at work in this world that do not want us to know what we are and are at work to diminish our unique human capabilities. For these forces we need to be predictable and controllable and at the same time believe that we are free and that our life is all that we choose it to be. It is brilliant in its subtlety and extremely effective and the chains become stronger with each passing generation. Experts and knowledge are used to convince us of the rightness of our path. And we fall for it every time, after all it is with our best interests at heart isn't it?

Foucault's work says it best –

> "This ready-made character of life comes from what Foucault calls disciplinary power or governmentality.....interacting with experts and authorities who are there to help me become a well-adjusted, happy, healthy productive member of society......central to this is the way it focuses attention on **me, you and everyone else as an object of both control and knowledge**...not governed in a way that represses or oppresses but in a way that feels best for me."
>
> – Michel Foucault

Maybe it is time that we open our eyes to what is really happening behind our backs not to get even or even show hate but to get humanity moving and to evolve onto becoming much more. To progress the human race not relying on technology although some does enhance the human species most does not, but rather to expand the human mind, heart and physical capabilities. Mastering our basic gifts that are lying dormant and unused. Some humans are evolving at a rapid rate whilst others are automatons. Time to choose which we will be. Conscious evolution is accelerating rapidly and it would be crazy to get caught sleeping through it.

Home sweet home is a good place to begin.

This undertaking is personal to each of us and the needs of each person living within the home need to be considered. It is no good escaping a regime of control and covert manipulation by replacing it with another set of rules and regulations. I will share with you how Julie and I have set up our home for success and some of our personal methods for replenishing our souls in our home which then become embodied and we can take out with us into the world.

I think it best to divide this section into three parts – **Defence – Inspiration – Ritual**.

Put simply this is our way of using our home for our own progress and self-improvement as opposed to being at the mercy of a system of forces, that condition our every thought if we allow it to happen. We control our exposure to any external influences that we consider to be tyrannical in nature or that contain the seeds of that intention and potential for mind manipulation. The more harmless they are depicted the more dangerous they are.

**Defence**

Most of you will think I am talking about defending our homes against intruders. It would be easy if that were the only defence needed. At least we would have a clear idea about the enemy and what their motives are. I am afraid the real foes masquerade as being on our side whilst at the same time trying at times successfully, to control our minds.

My thought is that we can structure our abode for ourselves and our loved ones to provide growth and development indefinitely. Currently our homes have been invaded by memes, mind viruses and we have lost control of having any choice as to what we want in our lives. You may be thinking I have lost my own mind and that this is all too tall a tale to take seriously, but I would implore you to do some research and begin with the following book –

## VIRUS OF THE MIND -*The New Science of the Meme* by Richard Brodie.

I first read this book about a decade ago and it became part of the process of gaining back my mind and my life that I now write about constantly. I suggest this book because this can be a confusing concept for conditioned people (us) to accept and this is as clear as you will find.

> *Virus of the Mind* exposes the imminent crisis of the dangerous new technology known as memetics. What is it, and how can we guard against its harmful effects? Our only chance is to have everyone read *Virus of the Mind* before it is too late. – Richard Brodie

97

**Please read it** and begin to understand exactly who your enemies may be in reality.

Brodie rather naively or diplomatically to sell his book takes the stance that much of the programming that happens is not meant and that it is the memes power not that of the human instigators that we should fear. I, on the other hand, believe that big business, particularly the pharmaceutical industry, the media, governments and religions all know what they are doing and they intend to exert their will on the masses for control and power. We are being enslaved and the power of these institutions is growing ever greater. We are much more than we know at this point and any limitations are induced via memes and programming. The simple answer to what are we and what exactly are our powers of the mind? is that we don't know but they are threatening enough to these malevolent forces to make them programme us away from discovering our true potential. What are they afraid of?

To begin I have shone the spotlight on memes as that is what we will be defending ourselves from. Harmful mind viruses. As a trained hypnotherapist I understand more than most how powerful our minds are and how crucial the mind is to the saving of the human race. We can use it for our benefit or continue to let others use our minds against us. This is the only choice we have to make. We are under the influence of mind viruses constantly and knowing this and where to look may arm us better in the fight for our freedom.

> *A meme is "an idea, behavior, or style that spreads from person to person within a culture". A meme acts as a unit for carrying cultural ideas, symbols, or practices that can be transmitted from one mind to another through writing, speech, gestures, rituals, or other imitable phenomena with*

*a mimicked theme. Supporters of the concept regard memes as the cultural equivalent to genes in that they self-replicate, mutate, and respond to forces. However, they do it much faster and can have an almost immediate effect.*

## TAKING BACK OUR MINDS

**Control the memes that organise your life and you control the quality of your life. We may, or may not ever be able to wrestle control of our minds away from our oppressors (big business corporations, religion, governments, the media etc) entirely but we can go a long way to re-gaining our freedom with a philosophy of re-programming and protection. Awareness is the key. Once we become aware of these forces and actually see what is going on behind our backs, it shines a light on it and we can rise above the destructive forces to wherever our destiny may lead once unencumbered by the fools that enslave us with their fear and greed.**

**The first meme we have to battle is the one that tells us that this is not true and that there is no threat. The choice is yours/ours.**

**All the answers we have ever sought are in our minds.**

Defending against such invisible forces could be considered impossible, but awareness is our biggest weapon. Or what we do with that awareness is at least our first choice. This is what I do. And what I do is changing constantly. Living the learning as I call it is a process of discovery and subsequent action to give myself the chance of progress and that priceless feeling of freedom. In a nutshell it is changing my mind under my terms as much as I possibly can.

We have been conditioned from birth for control and profit and the process continues in every moment with exposure for what passes for our world. We inadvertently sell our souls for a pile of shiny stuff believing we are limited and should be grateful for our lot in life as we deserve nothing more.

I am defending myself against damaging mind viruses (memes) in an attempt to know just how my mind works for myself. And maybe my oppressors are laughing and thinking that it is impossible and we have already lost, as we know not what they use to control us in reality. We can only guess and rely on pioneering members of our society to alert us to any new possibilities. I have been acting for some time now and the prognosis is good or at the very least better than being at the mercy of every Tom, Dick or Harry that wants to control our minds for profit or power.

Once I began to discover and minimise damaging memes and sow my own more progressive and personal memes, I began to reap the rewards. Mind is like body and responds to exercise, in fact a developed mind will lead your body to ever greater health and performance. And the disease and illness memes are just one of the ways we are kept living in fear. Gaining greater access to our subconscious mind (our true soul-mate) will change our lives. Helping us to understand the forces used against us, such as trance states (watching television) by using them for our benefit.

The next section will look at the power of auto-suggestion. Our whole life has been suggested to us and accepted by us.

**Give a person who has never had pot before a batch of brownies and tell them there is pot in them. Watch them act high!!**

*"The susceptibility of the modern(person) to pictorial suggestion enables advertising to exploit his lessened power of judgement."* – Johan Huizinga

**"*Self*-suggestion makes you master of yourself." – W. Clement Stone**

*"In almost every act of our daily lives, in all spheres of life, in our social contact and our ethical thinking. We are unknowingly dominated by a relatively small number of persons. It is they who pull the wires which control the public mind. Every thought we are fed creates our future for them."*
- Edward Bernays

**"Words: So innocent and powerless as they are, as standing in the dictionary, how potent for good and evil they become in the hands of one who knows how to combine them." – Nathaniel Hawthorne**

*"Like the wind that carries one ship east and another west, the law of auto-suggestion will lift you up or pull you down according to the way that you set your sails of thought." –* Napolean Hill

**"Just as you are unconsciously influenced by outside advertisement, announcement and appeal, so you can vitally influence your life from within by auto-suggestion. The first thing each morning, and the last thing each night, suggest to yourself specific ideas that you wish to embody in your character and personality. Address such suggestions to yourself, silently or aloud, until they are deeply impressed upon your mind." – Grenville Kleiser**

Autosuggestion is the most powerful tool that will help you gain control of your subconscious mind. It already shapes your life so you may as well learn how to make it work for you.

Maybe you need to develop faith in your own abilities.

**How to develop faith in your life?**

Faith is a state of mind that is created by repeated instructions to the subconscious.

Autosuggestion is telling your subconscious something so often and with such emotion that it believes what you tell it.

You can turn a lack of confidence (fear) into courage, through the aid of autosuggestion. Write, memorise and repeat that you have courage with positive emotions until your subconscious makes it a reality.

The law of autosuggestion will take you wherever you want to go, as long as you give the right directions. Which says that- If you realised how powerful your thoughts were you would never think a negative thought.

This is the biggest secret hidden in plain view and used to control a docile and distracted humanity. Much like shiny beads distracted the native Americans out of their rightful freedom, new technology is doing the same to billions of others now in this moment.

Autosuggestion is a powerful weapon with which one may rise to heights of great achievement, when it is used constructively. Used in a negative manner such as how we all make derogatory suggestions to ourselves and others constantly or used deliberately to control it will destroy all possibility of success, and as it is used continuously it will, and is actually destroying health and enslaving billions of people such as ourselves. Our conditioning is killing us.

The possibilities of thought training are infinite, it's consequences eternal, and yet few take the pains to direct their thinking into channels that will do them good, but instead leave all to chance and remain captive to our own forces used against us.

So now it is clear that my first line of defence is awareness and autosuggestion is number two. Defence is about protecting ourselves and our loves ones where possible from external suggestions or from our own self-deprecating suggestion that we, in all innocence, allow to infiltrate our minds. Only with our total awareness will we get to choose the contents of our own minds.

One would like to think that we are safe from invasive controlling suggestions within our homes. That assumption would be very wrong. Most, if not all of us have unwittingly invited our jailers to join us in our most private moments. If we were approached on the street with such suggestions we would ignore them or walk away and yet we allow our minds to be invaded while our guards are down in our homes, in the car and with the web via our tablets and phones. For some there is no escape.

Sanctuary – A place of refuge or safety. It is sad to feel the need for a sanctuary but it is an essential escape from a very turbulent and invasive world. This is how we (Julie and I) see our home. A place protected from the brainwashing onslaught. A place where memes can be controlled just a little and a place where we can create our own memes. These are some of our strategies for self-preservation.

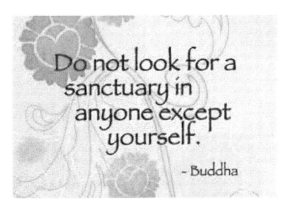

Do not look for a sanctuary in anyone except yourself.

- Buddha

We have a waste paper bin right next to the door. All unsolicited free papers, leaflets etc. go straight in the bin. Or on the ritual fires that we hold and you will hear about soon.

103

It is worth remembering that much of the time spent watching the television or listening to the radio we are in a trance state. With this in mind we do not watch commercial television or listen to commercial radio. We are very selective as to what we allow our minds to be exposed to. Reality shows, soaps and trashy talk shows airing peoples private live are all assigned to the metaphorical waste bin. No visual adds, no cold calling and no home visits from dogmatic religions from their legions of slaves that seem to want to talk about something that to all intents and purposes is agreed as being unknowable and unspeakable. I believe in the Tao, God, Being, the Life-force or whatever label you are comfortable with. I do not believe in religion. I do not welcome any person wishing to exert their primitive beliefs on me in my home and admit to asking them some very probing questions at times that sends them scurrying back down my drive. If I don't know the caller I do not accept calls, I avoid gossipy, opinionated people, although we don't seem to attract them these days. My social networking policy is that it is the spy in our homes but that it has its uses and we are helpless to avoid some invasion into our privacy that is what the so called war on terrorism has allowed. If it doesn't enhance our lives, then it is a waste of time. Social networking is mainly a waste of time. A distraction to add to the many other distractions but this one is harder to escape as it goes with us everywhere. I have heard mention that it won't be long before we are all chipped for our own safety. I am not so sure as we are gladly carrying tracking devices with us constantly now in a much more subtly and mutually agreed form. In fact, we pay for the privilege. The key point here is to avoid exposure to damaging memes at all costs. The price is just too high to pay. News and newspapers, all full of bullshit that we like to quote to each other until it becomes a new meme, our new opinion that we have read that morning. We only hear and read what our rulers deem is suitable for us to hear and see, what bends us to their will. Always a bias manipulative angle. Or more commonly pure lies. We would rather not know than have our world view shaped by the lies of fools. If you want to change the world, begin with yourself.

> # Believe nothing,
> no matter where you read it
> or who has said it, not even if
> i have said it, unless it agrees
> with your own reason and
> your own common sense.
> -Buddha

I know this all sounds impossible but that thought right there is just another mind virus. Having to have televisions, phones, the internet, fast food, cars, religions, drugs, alcohol and whatever else we are attached to are all memes, powerful mind viruses that keep us trapped in that world. None of that is true. And yet we pass it on to one another as truth. I wonder what our lives would be like stripped of all of the lies, are we sold illness every year? How much of illness is a meme. Can we actually heal ourselves and always have been able to but the drug industry needs us to spend fortunes on drugs in order for the global economy to line the pockets of our rulers. Every area of our lives is open to question. It is fun aye?

I know the changes are difficult to ingest but that is all part of the strength of the mind viruses that we are infected with. My meagre defences have evolved and will continue to evolve. My best defence is the new memes I am creating in my mind and spreading with this book. They may not have the staying power to fight the existing ones but I will keep trying. My mind continues to evolve. If we were looking after our physical health and safety, we would eliminate threats. It is the same when protecting your mind. Learn what the threats may be and do the best we can to counteract those threats and be mindful of where they come from.

The television is an obvious source of damaging mind viruses but I wish to mention two others that we are exposed to when we are in trance states. The first is commercial radio wherever you may be, particularly in your car when you are "miles away" (trance). The second is at the gym or anywhere else that commercials are played constantly. When we are in trance we are more susceptible to suggestions fired at us from a non-stop barrage of sound and vision. The repetitive commercial breaks on any media are equivalent to short hypnosis sessions as is much of your total viewing and listening time. Take note of the damaging suggestions via the ads, announcements and appeals that we, and our significant others are exposed to in the moments when our guard is down and we are oblivious to what is going on behind our backs. Observe your day in order to see how you are trained to respond to triggers with related behaviour.

An everyday example from my life – We purchased a pizza for delivery and subsequently receive offers via text at regular intervals. Not thinking a whole lot about it as it is such a mundane occurrence we responded on three more occasions which in itself is a rare occurrence. Take away food is an extremely unusual event for us as we are so well set up in our eating habits. I eventually took notice and realised that we had been trained as customers and were ordering pizza as they demanded with their offers coming in at times we were hungry and maybe feeling a little lazy and not as we would have chosen in our normal routine. On the last occasion I received the text, which planted the seed in my mind, and a few days later in a moment of weakness we ordered pizza. It was on this occasion that the penny dropped for us and we realised that we did not even enjoy the food that much it was more a promise of something special and it was not that special in reality. Our response was a conditioned response. We requested removal from the system and not had a pizza since or even thought about or discussed pizza.  Out of sight out of mind. That may seem quite trivial, but we are all constantly at risk from suggestion from many sources even our well-meaning friends and family often repeat suggestions they have been infected with as their own beliefs when in reality they are also victims of stunting suggestions keeping them stuck and preventing progress and self-improvement. Imagine if our situation were repeated constantly in an obese family setting and all of the heart break and trauma that that entails. It is made light of but that making light is the first meme that we need to change.

This is how we are controlled and manipulated even at a relatively low level by local businesses that should really carry a health warning. We are convinced we are limited or that we need such and such a product, we are not and we do not. Negative suggestions (mind viruses – memes) that we are fed and too readily accept limit our potential and development across the board and we dare not stand up and be different to the others in forging our own life path. That includes social, occupational, intellectual, environmental, spiritual and physical. There are damaging memes and norms in all areas and we contain all we need to succeed in all of these areas if we can just have the courage to discover for ourselves and create a few new memes that suit us better. The place to begin is by being aware of these memes and to defend against them wherever possible and to not accept them as truth. Defending our homes and then using our homes as inspiration for our reprogramming is the next section I will share with you.

> *Governments use mind control to control our every movement. The trick is to make people (us) think we have a choice. We are engaged in one sided psychological warfare each time we walk down the high street, enter a supermarket, open a magazine or newspaper, turn on the television or pc or listen to the radio. Becoming aware enables, us to protect our psyches and use the same weapons for our own benefit and the benefit of mankind. Memes can be defeated and reprogrammed.*

 **Inspiration**

So, how now to make any home – sweet – home an inspiration. Can home - sweet - home change our lives and inspire us to progress and throw off the shackles of our conditioning? Julie and I think the answer is a resounding yes.

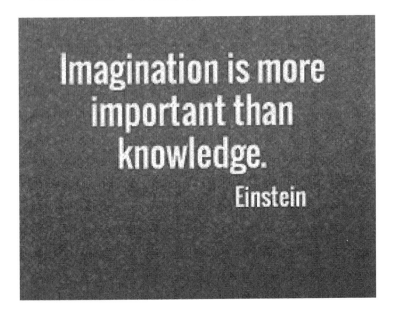

**Using Imagination to Add Value to Our Lives –**

Oscar Wilde stated

*"Nowadays people know the price of everything and the value of nothing".*

This I believe is the secret to finding some happiness in our personal worlds. It is as true today as it was when he said it, maybe even more so as consumerism and distraction become more deeply engrained in the human psyche and established as normal behaviours.

Most of us focus on the price and fail to see any value. What we need are tools in our lives that change our perspective and enable us to both attribute and recognise the value all around us.

This perspective requires some lifestyle change and an open mind. But the changes are well worth it as they will inspire us on to even greater change.

To attribute, discover, understand and appreciate value is to know the meaning of life.

What follows are my honest and quirky ways that I use to add value to my life and the blueprint I use when consuming (buying), does the purchase enhance the lives of Julie, myself maybe others? If not, then there is no purchase. Much of this takes us back to the innocence of our childhood and to a world of wonder and awe.

I implore you never to consider yourself too old to use your imagination to enhance your life. Learn from the children and return to a world with so much more potential and fun. Consider the possibility that we lose at least as much as we gain by growing up and becoming socialised. In many ways the uninhibited and natural inclination of the young is where true wisdom is to be found.

Our minds have naturally been closed off to anything that might threaten the status quo for our slave masters. Any behaviour that can be labelled as not normal is automatically shut out. But that is where we are going to find all of the new exciting stuff and start to realise that we have been lied to and are even inadvertently buying into and spreading lies ourselves. Our biggest challenge is to open our minds and dance with life in ways that feel okay for us whether they fit the norms or not. A world in which being called a daft bugger, crazy, quirky or that you have some funny ideas is the biggest compliment another person can pay you and a sign that you are finally behaving authentically away from the herd. Here Are some of our quirky methods that we use to fill our lives with beauty and the all-important meaning we all hunger for.

We set up and animate our home. Everything we own has a name and we endow our stuff with meaning and spirit. Everything in our world has value above and beyond the price. There are lessons and stories surrounding us all over our home.  This is great fun and fosters a great attitude towards everything that we include in our lives.

Most people look forward to naming a new pet or their new baby, we name everything, and not with the latest name for status but for what it means to us personally. That is why for me nicknames often have more value than names chosen early in our lives. Nicknames know something of who we are and are descriptive way beyond our birth names. Nicknames are often given by those that are close and can see the real self when it peeps out or before it is buried for ever under fake identities. I have a multitude of nicknames for Julie all of them based on much more than a name and are shared as so much more than a word.

You will need to be in your most receptive mode, abandoning your sensible, conditioned robot brain and ready to take a leap back into the world of possibilities, wonder and awe.

For something to enhance your life is needs to be functional. For instance, a picture of your grandchildren is life enhancing whereas the latest 'must have' piece of technology probably isn't. A small well thought out token of somebody's appreciation, as a way of saying thanks for a situation, contains the reason in the gift and as such has tremendous value, but an expensive gift bought on a day suggested by others with very little thought is probably not going to contain that much needed value. And may well be forgotten very quickly by both parties. This is a big reason why I hate the commercial gift buying days. There is no thought in buying the set gifts on these "special" gift days just because if you do not you will be labelled as uncaring for your omission. Your big heart for the rest of the year will be ignored as you are pressured into buying on the exact day determined by people that you cannot even see. Does that not sound a bit like we are being cajoled into buying when others want us to buy? I for one feel resentful of these days of forced consumerism and consider it criminal that days such as xmas day have turned into a mandatory expenditure day for us all. Consider the situation and how devious the whole situation is and know that we are controlled at all times in similar ways and many of us even argue to be controlled this way because there is some shiny stuff to be gained and some partying to be indulged in. We sell our freedom for shiny gadgets and the promise of a great day that if we are honest never really materialises as we all sit fed up once the anti-climax has been fully realised. We then look forward to the next planned "happy" time that will have the same effect. Conveniently such occasions are spaced throughout the year so that we are permanently distracted and never stop to question what the hell is happening with our lives and how much of our lives can actually be claimed to be ours. And how much of our authentic self is involved in living our lives.

In a nutshell it is the thought that counts but not the thought to buy the gift, rather the thought that transcends the gift buying experience. That is why gifts on commercial gift buying occasions such as valentines, mother's day, father's day, Easter and other such "profit making" fake days are such a waste of time in my opinion. Break the mould and buy gifts for people when you want to and not when you are told to. I won't get started on Xmas. When was the last time you bought a gift just because you thought of another and you wanted to let them know how much you are grateful for their presence in your life. Even a card with more than the usual minimal greetings inside can work wonders. Fill the card with your own personal writing that can be such a lift to the person receiving it. A letter can be even more gratifying. A lost art that needs to be rekindled, if you are thinking that you can't write letters then that is all the more reason to start. Once you begin you will need extra paper. Trust me when I say that when you know somebody well, the words will eventually flow like water.

A gift for yourself is a great thing to do, but can we make the gift functional and imbue it with meaning and value from the start.

At the same time this process creates new memes throughout our home and we undergo a reprogramming away from the mind viruses that were keeping us stuck in a state of mind that was not serving us well.

I will begin with my three dogs, all with one syllable names for ease of calling. Jake, Smudge and Zing. Names that suit them to a tee. We name all of our house plants and they do thrive when endowed with an identity which changes our intention to them. I gauge the energy and flow in our home by the health of our plants. I will not get into it too deeply here but if you are interested I suggest you search for research done by a man named Backster about plants and how amazing they may actually be. We always talk to the plants and the dogs, in fact we will talk to anything, the car (Hermes), my bike (Tao) and even the television which I have named Siren as it has the ability to lure humans onto the rocks and destroy them. Since writing this I have got rid of the television. It should carry a government health warning but then they would have to admit that it is a weapon used in the war to control the minds of the masses. Incidentally, Julie's bike is called Bella and she does seem to have less mechanical problems since she named her. A name automatically fosters a better relationship with anything. It is probable that Julie treats Bella better than she would her nameless bike thing. That is how it has panned out, before the naming Julie had many problems and the number of flat tyres was becoming a standing joke. Since? There does seem to be more flow to the relationship and less issues. Quirky? Yes, but just because we don't understand something fully is no reason to shut ourselves off from the possibilities. We know nothing and the sooner we accept we have much to learn the wiser we will be.

We work to bring our homes alive with beauty and meaning, filling our lives with creative positive memes. This is great fun and such an education and reminder of some of the important things in life. Our home tells a story but a story that is ever changing and a process as opposed to a fixed myth. I fully expect it comes alive behind our backs, much like a movie, leading a double life of animation and the expected life of inanimate things when being watched or in the presence of nonbelievers.

At first visitors thought that our stuff was bought purely to amuse the grandchildren. I can safely say everything in this house has been purchased with our psyches in mind and if that seems to suit the children also, then I am happy to be in their gang.

I would just like to take this opportunity to suggest some further reading relevant to this section.  If you are intending to prise your mind wide-open then this is the kind of book you simply must read.

*The Nature of Things – The secret Life of Inanimate Objects*

By Lyall Watson

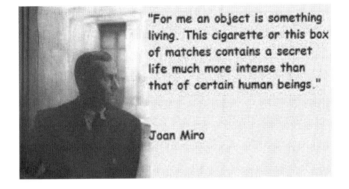

"For me an object is something living. This cigarette or this box of matches contains a secret life much more intense than that of certain human beings."

Joan Miro

**The Seven Dwarves mythology** – We have two ornaments that show the seven dwarves – popular theory proposes that the dwarves were projections of the traits that snow white lacked in herself. An attraction of opposites, much like Julie and myself as discussed in my book Chilled Demons and Cheeky Heroes. Our psyche has a tendency to try to become complete and is quite happy to cheat by finding the missing pieces in another person. This all happens unconsciously and with great power and attraction. Snow white was very happy with her dwarves because she had found what was buried in herself. However, she would at some time need to find those traits in herself rather than depend on others. Nevertheless, a very good choice of life partners. Snow White also had personality qualities that the dwarves lacked such as nurturing, kindness, and caring. When I say lacked what I really mean is that those qualities although present in us all were the inferior qualities for the seven dwarfs. The projection was two-way and everybody gained from the experience.

I like this theory but I also think that prince charming represents the ideal and the conformist thing to do was to match up with him. I imagine that the relationship with the prince was very shallow and once the initial excitement played out there was very little to keep them together. As with all ideals, norms and conformist choices they are not always based on a very strong foundation. It seems to be more about what others want or what is good for appearances than any heart felt action. Which is possibly why so many relationships are doomed to failure in the 21st century. I see snow white as being happier with her seven lovable dwarfs.

Humour me for a moment and imagine the seven dwarves as one very authentic person. Do you see how snow white would have been much happier with that person than the life that she actually chose. There is so much more to that person than to the ideal of a prince charming in my mind and that is what I get from my seven dwarves, a real down to earth relationship based on much more than looks and charm. Was that the lesson for us to learn. I think so, now you can watch your children's films with a new awareness and a search for meaning and truth that can only be found in mythology. Life can be filled with personal meaning. Let's continue on.

Julie and I decided to see if we could name the dwarfs that we represent for each other. After eventually getting past the stinky and farty name calling stage we did come up with a few. Julie would contain for me the following -> Busy, Dancey, Dopey, Happy, Risky and not too surprisingly I would be mostly the opposite -> Sleepy, Not-Dancey, Dopey, Grumpy and Careful. I did suggest to Julie that the main reason she has me in her life is because she needed lots more grumpiness to balance out her happy optimistic personality. True to type she replied "You're not grumpy" – Bless her. You can have some fun with this. Try It!

| | | |
|---|---|---|
| Grouchy | Gabby | Fearful |
| Sleepy | Smiley | Jumpy |
| Hopeful | Shy | Droopy |
| Dopey | Sniffy | Wishful |
| Puffy | Dumpy | Sneezy |
| Lazy | Pop | Grumpy |
| Bashful | Cheerful | Teach |
| Shorty | Nifty | Happy |
| Doc | Wheezy | Stubby |

**Beaky, Mick and Titch** are three chimpanzees sitting on each other's shoulders, standing about 3ft high. Hear no, speak no, see no evil. The reason for these guys is a reminder of how readily we all seem to be to judge and gossip about others. With work we can stop this behaviour that is mostly just a case of not thinking before we speak rather than any deeply held beliefs. In the past I have thought or said something derogatory about a person and then realised that I do not even agree with myself. Eventually wondering where the comment came from. Was it just a learned standard reply or my shadow side showing me a part of myself that I needed to accept and deal with accordingly. I am sure it is the latter and that is a good thing because it still leaves me in control of my actions, albeit a side of myself that does seem to act before I get the chance to think. I have since worked on giving myself time to think and reprogramming my mind away from destructive mind viruses, the memes, that I am programmed with. All that is needed is awareness of what is happening in our own minds and the effort to choose new thoughts. Thoughts better suited to what we hold dear. Have you ever noticed that if you are in a mood and being grumpy and judgmental about others and about life in general, life and others seem to mirror your sentiments back at you in physical form? A bad day originates inside with your thoughts. I have no doubt.

**Socrates** – is a large stern and muscular gargoyle, one of many gargoyles I have in my home. For me gargoyles depict protection, the fact that beauty is in the eye of the beholder and so much more. Gargoyles have a bad public image that has been manipulated by forces wishing to benefit from the existence of evil for the benefit of their own gains.

Socrates is both intellectual and physically powerful. He epitomises both brains and brawn. We do not have to be one or the other and we all can quite happily aspire to contain both physical and intellectual skills. Casting off the feeble professor and dumb jock labels. We are all both, all that is needed is an acceptance of that fact. Socrates is a vegetarian pacifist. It is commonly quoted that we can't judge a book by its cover and yet we do exactly that and at the same time spend billions of our money and many hours of our time on our own covers so that we give just the right impression. The ideal. Whatever that may be? Very often losing any uniqueness we may possess in order to look like all the others. I wonder if it might be more prudent to spend time and money on developing and discovering our uniquely individual contents rather than embellishing our covers any further. It is our social conditioning that leads us to judge others and ourselves as not good enough. A ploy designed to limit our development. However, this ploy is having the positive effect of making us question whether we are more than we have been taught to believe and is leading to an opposing culture that contains memetics, the law of attraction, Morphic field research and other areas that are expanding human consciousness way beyond what we have been brainwashed to believe previously. There is a gap between the new thinkers and mainstream dogma that is widening every day and all that is needed is to open up our minds to anything as possible. This is out of the question to many but open mindedness will spread as a meme just like any other meme. Eventually and with good fortune life affirming memes that expand human consciousness will win out over the diminishing memes being used to enslave us. The battle has begun as now both sides are aware that there is one. And the advantage of our oppressors has lessened as our misplaced faith in them has waned. This book is just one small example of the new thinking. An example that sits somewhere in between the extremes but is on the move to creating ways of producing positive memes in our lives at a level that we can all achieve with ease and some fun.

**Toby,** another gargoyle is squatting menacingly atop a dome on a column, he looks full of mischief and devilment. Toby is a reminder that we all have that edgy mischievous side to our personalities often conditioned out of us when we are young. We should honour that side of our psyches. Often known as the trickster archetype.

Currently my granddaughter typifies that type, I call her the rock star. But alas I await the day that she "grows" out of it or more to the point buries it deep inside as being unacceptable to her in society. I will watch with interest as her less acceptable traits get buried as her shadow continues to form.

**Michel** – another gargoyle. Michel has a ball and chain attached to his leg and serves as a reminder of how we are all subject to subtle knowledge and power forces that serve to limit us in our development and freedom. Named after Michel Foucault who was a pioneer in observing and identifying these forces in his work.

My final gargoyle is **Hemlock**. Hemlock sits on a throne with a very thoughtful pose. A thinker. I often wonder just what he may be thinking about as he sits next to my desk. I imagine him a member of a minority group with no real power and judged for his looks and illusory fears about what his kind are at the core of their nature. Being different leaves many stranded in a world of prejudice and cruelty and we only have to consider the plight of different races over human history and maybe the most maligned of all, the female of our species, who as women are still to this day treated with an inequality and cruelty that shames the human race.

**Nobby** – a Senex (wise elder) figure is my nature wanderer. A reminder of how we are all seeking to reconnect with something deep inside of us that we have lost contact with. Maybe it can be found in nature away from distractions more than anywhere else. It begins with precious moments of bliss and expands as we feel the urge to live more in the flow. Both in our moments in nature and within mainstream life. We all know how it feels when our minds are right and it feels like the whole world wants what we want. That is the flow. Once felt it is conspicuous by its absence and we feel the need more and more. Our insides are in harmony with our outsides and we know that what I am saying is true just because we can feel it and know it is real. Nobby is my guide, and he is aided by my next figure.

**Gaia** is mother earth in its totality.

> *For many, a spirituality of the Earth has quickly become equated with Gaia worship – Gaia is the name of the ancient Greek goddess of the Earth, and as a name it was recently revived to refer to the hypothesis formed by James Lovelock and Lynn Margulis, who postulate that the whole biosphere*

*may be alive in that the Earth's life forms are themselves responsible for regulating the conditions that make life on the planet possible. One living breathing organism.*

**Robert Lanza's book Biocentrism continues with the theme.**

**A must read to add to your growing list -**

*"The whole of Western natural philosophy is undergoing a sea change again, forced upon us by the experimental findings of quantum theory. At the same time, these findings have increased our doubt and uncertainty about traditional physical explanations of the universe's genesis and structure.*

*Biocentrism completes this shift in worldview, turning the planet upside down again with the revolutionary view that life creates the universe instead of the other way around. In this new paradigm, life is not just an accidental by-product of the laws of physics.*

*Biocentrism takes the reader on a seemingly improbable but ultimately inescapable journey through a foreign universe— our own—from the viewpoints of an acclaimed biologist and a leading astronomer. Switching perspective from physics to biology unlocks the cages in which Western science has unwittingly managed to confine itself. Biocentrism shatters the reader's ideas of life, time and space, and even death. At the same time, it releases us from the dull worldview that life is merely the activity of an admixture of carbon and a few other elements; it suggests the exhilarating possibility that life is fundamentally immortal.*

*Biocentrism awakens in readers a new sense of possibility and is full of so many shocking new perspectives that the reader will never see reality the same way again."*

As you can see the value that I attribute to Gaia in my home is colossal and it will be ever changing as I read more revealing books on the subject and my world view continues to evolve. In my home Gaia is depicted as a loving mother nature. And as a reminder that all of nature may be dependent on all of life and that whenever we harm the planet we are in fact harming ourselves as a species on the planet. Another book is – **Rupert Sheldrake's book on Morphic Fields – The Science Delusion.** Another must read that will amaze any reader with what may be possible in our lives once the limiters are discovered and are then gradually disabled.

**The Thinker** (Rodin) – Living life to the full is the phrase that I am reminded of when I see my thinker figure. In our society it is thought that to live life to the full you must be doing something and full of activity and wanting. That is simply not true for everyone and those of us that are inclined to introversion can live a very full life within ourselves. We live in an extraverted world and it has taken me a long time to allow myself to live my life in my own way and according to my personality traits. My inner life is indeed rich and amazing, and just as thrilling for me as a visit to an amusement park may be for an extravert. It is the same for passion. Passion for me is a deep internal drive that may not be seen often by observers but is nonetheless a very powerful force. I love to observe extraverts enjoying their external world to the maximum but I just no longer feel that I should be doing the same and there must be something wrong with me. On the flip side I get very excited (not obviously maybe) by one to one contact or maybe even time alone in nature or with a good book. And when presented with ideas and possibilities I am veritably brimming over with good feelings. And after all of the years of feeling different I now allow myself to be myself and I see many others with a similar personality either trying to be something they are not or accepting of themselves and happy in their internal paradise. I urge all of my more extravert readers to understand that even though you may not be able to see an introverts bliss it is as real to them as your more obvious "living life to the full" is to you. This is what the thinker (Rodin) means to me. I imagine him as living his life to the full, deep in contemplation. I also think that Rodin's thinker is thinking original thoughts and that he doesn't just accept the ideas and thoughts handed down to him by the media or so called experts that materialise any time we have to be convinced of some "fact" or other easy to come by "truth". These invariably prove to be lies packaged to manipulate an end result for the forces at work that do not have our best interests at heart but rather work for the Gods of profit and control. Ultimately keeping the masses enslaved with false knowledge where there were once chains. However, all of that being said I am aware that I really need to work on getting out more and socialising. The sarcastic saying "you need to get out more" is spot on with me.

**Eros** – is a small cherub figure, squatting down and holding in his hand a snail that he looks at with innocent interest, wonder and awe. For me Eros is symbolic of the essence of life and the priceless values of childlike wonder and awe that we seem to have lost, becoming desensitised to the wonders of the natural world and the simple precious moments that can fill our day if only we can or will awaken from our technologically led stupor.

I have an Escher print on canvass that is an eye with a skull in the centre looking out. For many it is interpreted as the shadow presence. I think it could equally be our true self. However, it is interpreted it is a reminder that there is far more to us than we are led to believe. We are energy. Solidity is an illusion, a trick of the light. My Escher prompts me to thinking about what we really are and how amazing are our minds to co-create all that we experience with the Tao, God or the life force.

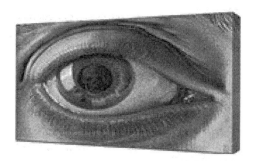

**Wally The Werewolf and The Incredible Hulk** – Another theme that I feel is important for us as human beings to be mindful of is the presence of a darker side within us all. Wally and The Hulk would have been joined by a Dr Jekyll and Mr Hide character if I could have found one. These are great myths and stories that act as a reminder for me of all that we contain and how a loving acceptance of ourselves, warts and all is the only way to progress.

 Ritual

When you attach ritual to your thoughts via some sort of ceremony, it becomes sacred and even the smallest ritual seems to help impress the thoughts deep within the psyche. Feelings are enhanced. Ritual recognises something larger than ourselves as part of the plan. That is the same whatever label we use for our God, Tao or life force. Adding ritual is adding meaning to the goals and intentions, it sets something (energies) in motion.

There are rituals that we have introduced into our lives that serve to reinforce the process of change and aids us in breaking free from old conditioning that we feel serves us poorly. We have found that by introducing a new habit as a ritual, at least initially, it seems to harden the new habit and the changes become more concrete and enduring. Even something as basic as saying affirmations at set times. Most of these have just evolved from my thoughts and behaviours but there are some that I have modified from the ideas of others. There are very few totally new ideas and there will be remnants of other rituals in our simple ceremonies.  Many think that fire is a destructive force, that is totally misguided as energy can't be destroyed. Fire is a transforming element, transforming energy from a relatively inert resting phase into a more dynamic flowing phase. We use fire in our daily letting go ritual. An amazing element. It all begins with thoughts and then those thoughts take the shape of words, emotions and images. For me the words feel as if they are the instigator and as such the affirmations emerging from my thoughts and ideas take centre stage. How can we increase the value of our words to illicit feelings that will turbo charge those words. The key ingredients in all rituals are the words and intentions and these are contained in the affirmations, meditations or prayers.

positive thoughts
generate
positive feelings
and attract
positive life
experiences

## Affirmations – Thought vibrations change lives

It is my firm belief that our minds create the realities that we live out in the material world. That means that I think the law of attraction, cosmic ordering, the power of prayer and all of the other names given to the use of invisible energy to create our worlds are totally valid and skills to be mastered. I also believe that our ruling classes know that this is true and our conditioning is designed to keep us from our true potential. We are easier to control as limited docile beings. This universal force is God, the Tao, Life force, whatever the label it is the same mystery that we are all constantly perplexed by. We all have separate theories and ideas for the exact same power in the universe and as we evolve we are increasingly able to manipulate this power as some remarkable individuals do and many more are learning to do. At the heart of this power it is much more than a get rich quick scheme, but it may well be that the leaders in the field end up being those that are more fuelled with wanting more stuff than saving the world but they may just save the world in the process. The greedy among us may be leading the way. It is interesting to observe the evolution of this truth as it accelerates into the beliefs of more and more people. There are always ironies in any process and this is just the case here. The motivation to have more will lead us to understanding that less or enough has always been the answer.

**Simple But Effective Affirmation**
Repeat the affirmation "I love myself" at least a thousand times daily. Use a counter if necessary. It will take max 25 minutes. You will definitely see positive changes in your life in 2-3 months. Make it a lifelong habit.

One of the main tools for controlling the thought vibrations produced is by using heart felt affirmations and suggestions. This can be specific affirmations we take on for the purpose of change, prayer, hypnotic suggestions or just the endless mind chatter that goes on each day, mostly unwitnessed, inside of us all. I have talked much about suggestion and repetition. The purpose of all of these habits is to rewrite our programmed minds. It is that simple. Trance states and repetition are two of the methods used to speed up the process. It does seem that one of the effects of our evolving consciousness is that we are abler to change our current robotic programming than we have been previously and I see no reason to think that this will not progress even further as more positive (outside the box thinking, but there is a new box) memes are created by positive people. This is the conscious evolution. More people will be attracted to new thinking and the old memes will be exposed as the controlling weapons that they are, weakening them into extinction. The hope is that eventually the new thinking will become the norm and mankind will be saved. Cool aye?

How can we help? By changing the way we think and making it permanent change away from the old bullshit but remaining open-minded to any new evolving ideas. Otherwise we will be the future dogmatic generation. We do not want that. Change it would seem is constant and even the surest facts eventually fade into being the stepping stones within change that they were always intended to be.

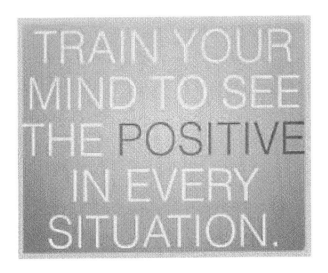

Our thought vibrations will change our lives and affirmations are a part of that process. The only obstacle is us and our current belief system. Resistance only stops progress and is futile. Would it be better to know that we have tried and failed with affirmations than we let our resistance to change stop us before we get started?

Even the most disciplined spiritual seeker affirming throughout the day may still be losing out to negative thoughts, judgements and complaints that pervade our minds when our guard is down. The practise of affirming does fill time that might be spent in our default negative thinking as we can only think one thought at a time. Positive affirmations are a great way of becoming positive if we are aware that we are in a negative moment. That is where awareness is vital. The process is one of progress rather than immediate reprogramming. Recognising that we control our beliefs can be a big step in our evolution. It is not things in themselves that contain our opinions but rather how we have been conditioned to look at them. Rain and sunshine for instance. Neither is necessarily better or worse than the other but how we look at each creates a very different attitude to each. Work, rest and play is another example. Currently work is a necessary evil for most whilst weekends, breaks and holidays are all good. Rising in the morning for most is a chore to go to work but great to meet for some fun. None of this is real but merely how we perceive things in our worlds. A world that seems to want to keep us in negative mode. Just look at the world (bad) news and most of our viewing. If we can learn to love the rain and the sunshine equally then we can pretty much change anything in our lives once we become aware we are able to do that. Incidentally your reaction to my suggesting love for rainy days is a good gauge of how deeply the conditioning goes. If you live in a dry desert area, then maybe you already love the rain and sunny days are your greater evil. But you get the picture it is not things in themselves but the way we look at them that dictates our state of mind. My dog Jake is noisy and disobedient when I think he is. No surprise there but when I change those thoughts he is like a little angel. Jake is one of my practise areas. Another area of concern for me was waking up as Mr Grumpy every morning. I can thank Pam Grout for the suggestion of playing myself happy tunes first thing and bopping around for breaking that great expectation. I now expect to feel happier in the morning. Pam's books E squared and E cubed are great and well worth a read. She depicts the perfect world that we can achieve if we can just get over the bullshit social control conditioning that keeps us from discovering our limitless potential. I seriously believe that "Ignore it and it will go away" could ultimately be the best strategy for overcoming such negative influences on our lives. I would say the same for illness but that is an emotionally laden subject for many and I could be accused of treating it too lightly. But lightly is exactly how we should treat it, rather than making illness part of our expectations and attaching it to our identities. However, the solution could be as simple as changing the way we view our health at the same time as we change the rest of our thoughts about less emotionally charged subjects.

Complaints are negative affirmations. They are affirmations of things we don't really want in our lives. But by constantly moaning and complaining we affirm more of whatever we are moaning about into our lives. That is not very cool at all. It does explain why the complaining party continues to be plagued by the same issues. By constantly complaining we reinforce problems, making them much harder to replace with the positive choice. I know the stuff I complain about never changes. Until the penny drops and I realise what I have been doing and focus on that area of my development until the new non-complaining Adam is the default subconscious reaction to the issues being addressed. Don't be fooled. What you chose to think about all day is what you are going to get. If you choose to continue to complain and focus on the problems and adversity that is abundant in our cultures and in the media particularly, that is what you are going to attract to your life.

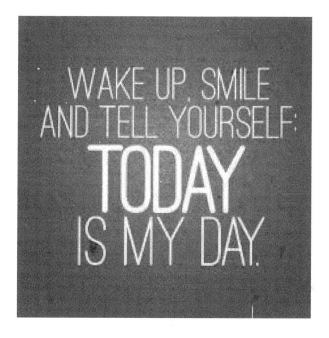

Create a positive atmosphere. Stay happy (affirm it), smile and laugh often and be kind to others be the epitome of a positive loving person. Live in a personal wonderland and let positivity surround and protect your positive statements. That is whether you feel like it or not. Fake it until you make it. You will never get rid of all negative thoughts. But don't worry as your average thought will be more positive and that will bring good vibes and good results. And at least you are noticing those pesky negative grumblings. We have 60,000 thoughts a day, mostly negative if left untended so progress is guaranteed but perfection is unlikely. The odds are in our favour. Just nip any negativity in the bud once you become aware to avoid a landslide of negative thoughts following and burying you in the rubble. You will find certain situations are more likely to promote negativity in you, such as watching the television or shopping in the sales. Avoid them. You are not missing anything. Wherever you feel that there may be viruses of the mind (negative or damaging thoughts) just make sure you are not present to be infected at least until you are so strong that they just serve to strengthen your resolve to be positive. You will see them for what they are and they will have no effect on your core level of positivity. I have noticed that negative thoughts can also attack when I am alone and sitting quietly. It is strange and I have no clue what prompts this sneak attack. At first I would be buried in these thoughts before I became aware but as time has passed I am much more adept at shrugging and letting the thought pass. Resistance is futile and will only strengthen the negative, as anger and frustration at negative thoughts is just piling more negativity on the fire. The exact opposite is required, a loving shrug and an acceptance until you can gather some positive affirmations suitable to your situation. You will have favourites and some that you can call on in an emergency. I have five words that can stabilise my mood in an instant and roll off the tongue.

***I am Happy, Healthy, Wealthy, Healed and Whole.***

I have each word loaded with value in my mind.

If you decide on a more optimistic world view. Seeing good all around you, knowing you will attract prosperity and reciting positive affirmations whenever possible You will be gobsmacked at how situations can transform from crap to wonderful. It just takes a little concerted conscious effort and some self-discipline. You only have to choose and follow through with positive action.

The general idea of affirmations is that by speaking, writing and reading them we change our thought process to an emotionally charged higher level. I will add thinking them to that list. Feeling an affirmation seems to be an important part of the process and I think that is why the happy music in the morning works so well. The happy lyrics are the affirmation but when combined with the music the result is a feeling not just words or music. The sum of the parts is what makes this effective. It produces the feeling of wanting to dance, (more jumping really) even in me, and brings a smile to faces. Particularly to Julie when she sees me dancing.

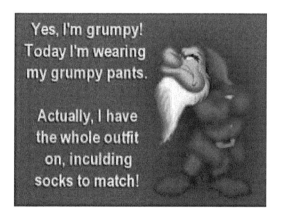

That would seem to be an extremely contagious affirmation. I can vouch for an increase in happiness in the mornings for Mr Grumpy.

In fact, I am going to rename myself now and lose that label forever. I am now the man formerly known as Mr Grumpy.

No! That doesn't work. I will be Mr Happy, even though I can feel the resistance to that new name due to my taking on the label of Mr Grumpy for so many years. Surely I can't be Mr Happy? Yep, that's me, Mr Happy. Do you see how this works? We can reinvent ourselves. We are reinventing ourselves. That is how change happens.

# HAPPINESS IS

...dancing
like idiots.

With repetition and practise this in turn overwrites negativity even negativity spoken in jest and attracts a healthier attitude to life which creates a better life for the individual. No longer accepting that we are helpless to forces from outside and that we can change anything we want to work at.

As with any inner mind work we have to have 100% faith in the process and quiet our inner cynic that will most assuredly have much to say. It is our conscious beliefs aligning with our deep subconscious (great) expectations that ultimately create our life experience.

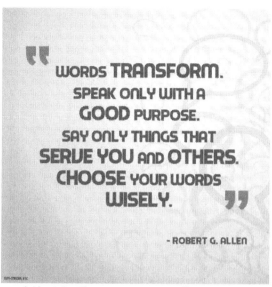

There is a snag and that is that we are totally unaware of those subconscious (great) expectations. However, as we are here desiring change we can assume they are not aligning with our positive conscious intentions just at this moment. Our actual deep relatively unknown expectations, whatever they may be are what sabotage our progress.

We desire change. Maybe at first in just one area of our lives that highlights us being out of step, a feeling of being out of flow, but not really being able to put our finger on any particular change in the rational world. Enter affirmations, hypnotherapy and many other personal progress tools. We enter looking for a quick fix and inadvertently embark on the most important and yet mysterious journey of our lives. Attempting to know our real self and understanding what is going on in the world that for so many years we thought we had all of the answers to. It is tough to find out that we know nothing and the world is nothing like we thought it was up to this point.

Highly emotionally charged words (affirmations) are what we wish to use to re-programme our existing expectations. We wish these greater and more fitting expectations to become our new default setting for running our lives. But this time we want to choose the thoughts and beliefs that best shape our lives.

I have used affirmations with some success but like many others before me have found that repeating somebody else's words can feel impersonal and if I am doubting the process my mind will not change. Whatever we decide to affirm needs to be intellectually believable to me in my current mind set and preferably have some emotion attached to it. We should feel a good affirmation. What is believable and emotional will change as we develop. It has changed for me. I will explain why. Prayer is Affirmation and often emotionally charged. I would mention that it is okay to make up your own prayers. Maybe ones that you understand fully the sentiment involved. I have my own version of the Lord's prayer that I use and I have in the past created many personal prayers. I used the Lord's prayer because I grew up with it and it has already got feelings attached from my childhood. I did feel it needed a more up to date feel for who I am now but it still has that rhythm and flow that is so important to that prayer. I just don't call them prayers to me they are all affirmations. And the Lord's Prayer is such a positive emotion filled affirmation of a relationship with the creative intelligence we have so many names for.

*I choose...*

to live by choice, not by chance;
to make changes, not excuses;
to be motivated, not manipulated;
to be useful, not used;
to excel, not compete;
I choose self esteem, not self pity.
I choose to listen to my inner voice,
not the random opinion of others.

## Choosing Your Thoughts

I have developed a personal method that you are free to use if you wish. If you feel it has value for you. I create emotionally charged words by increasing the value of the word for me, which can then be used in short affirmations. It is unnecessary to remember lots of long affirmations as the meaning is contained in the key word or value used in the sentence. I call this method choosing. It is something we can use every day and every way as stated by Emile Coue's famous "every day in every way I get better and better" affirmation. I still use that one. If it ain't broke don't fix it.

How does choosing work?

The first step is to choose words that we value, that feel right inside. The word has value to begin with and we then work to increase the value of our key words. Some value words are more obvious choices. The art is in the value word being loaded with positive, life affirming meaning and emotion that choosing the value ignites a thought process that can only mean progress. Moreover, we feel the value resonating throughout our whole being. Our value

140

word will contain as much information or positive baggage as we wish to include linked to a single word.

I will use some values that are very general and show how I deal with them. I have picked values that we all have an interest in developing.

### Choosing Money

An example affirmation – "**I choose money now.**" Short and sweet.

My value word is money and we can now develop the word money into a value free from fear and stigma. A value for which we can foster genuine subconscious great expectations to match our conscious intentions and expectations.

You will discover that the value of money would have had me running for cover in a cold sweat no so long ago. I had much work to do to create a feel good factor around the value of money.

What feelings does the word money contain for us and are the thoughts money creates helping or hindering our progress?

Sadly, and typically the less we have the more damaging may be our beliefs and expectations of ever having enough. A mind virus (meme) concerning money is that the rich get richer and the poor get poorer, this is a suggestion that is self-fulfilling and not based on any real truth when viewed from the world of our thoughts becoming our reality. However, it is far easier to imagine success and then let go from a position of wealth than it is from a needy, "barely making ends meet" situation. The thinking needs to change.

For me, at rock bottom the word money was a word that meant doubt, shame, helplessness and constant struggle. How have I turned it around? What follows are some of the facts that have made money a more acceptable, less fearful addition to my affirmation regime. When **"I choose money now"**, the words contain all of this information now and all that I learn as I get wiser will also become embedded in this small sentence that will contain multitudes. The word money triggers the following liberating thoughts for me at this point in my life.

My first thought is a realisation that the ruling classes, our oppressors know exactly how life and minds work and deliberately condition the masses (us) with the false belief that money is the road to happiness and the end of suffering when in actual fact worshipping money more often than not leads to fear disillusionment and more suffering. Buddhist thought is that the end of suffering comes with the end of desire (wanting and having). Our oppressors are always prepared to take our money as it is predictably drawn back to them by the various devices designed specifically for this purpose such as consumerism, taxes, fines and charity donations to help with problems that they should be dealing with instead of spending our money on arms. When we lose money through collapses of financial institutions, do our oppressors suffer? Never, they always seem to close ranks and take maximum benefit from our losses. I believe we are being kept from reaching our potential deliberately but I am still quite able to love and accept all of humanity because they do not really know what they are doing any more than we know how to break free but we are learning and I am sure the same can be said for them. I am confident that at some point in time we will all unite.

One truth might be that by taking the middle ground with money and understanding that any power money has is created by ourselves with a massive push from our oppressors for social control. This monster that is created is then the object of desire for billions as being the answer to all problems. There are no problems that money can't fix. And yet people that have it all still commit suicide regularly. Hmm! The desire for what it can buy added to a strong fear of what an extreme lack will mean create a very contradictory state of mind. Famine or feast. Neither of which will attract peace of mind or happiness or are in actual fact real situations. This imaginary situation which is held in the mind of billions produces a very anxious masses, a fearful population that can't stop earning, spending, borrowing and panicking. And at the same time financing the ruling classes lifestyle and future plans that we know nothing about. So! What is the answer?

Once more **The Golden Mean** or the middle ground is where the true power is for the majority of us. The aim is to develop a relaxed and grateful attitude to money without elevating it to a position in our lives where desire for more, more, more or fear of lacking can dominate our thoughts and reduce all that we do to its monetary value. The average month for most begins on pay day with a more stuff attitude and ends later in the month with a lacking state of mind. Even the most well off, spend all month with that having more attitude and the least well off spend all month lacking. This is a state of mind perpetuated by our capitalist society and the messages fired at us from the media and our gadgets 24 hours a day. It is not real.

**Whoever cultivates the golden mean avoids both the poverty of a hovel and the envy of a palace.**

Horace

QuoteAddicts

We wish to become high energy, receptive, manifesting masters and that cannot be achieved by stressing about having more or less money. It is funny that more money would make all of our lists and the only way to get it is to be indifferent about it. Got to love the The Universe, God, The Tao, Life Force etc.

I always smile when I think of two dog ornaments my Mum used to have at home when I was very young, they were kept on a shelf over the stairs and as I came down from my bedroom they were at eye level. Both standing as humans, upright and proud. The first well dressed and obviously wealthy was labelled "easy come". The second, a little dishevelled holding out his empty pockets and labelled "easy go", both smiling is how I remember them, as if they know the laws of the universe and the secret of an abundant life and the easy come attitude would pay off, from any start position. I like to think the easy go figure turned his life around with his easy come smiling attitude. They should have both been labelled "Easy Come". We will do well to adopt an easy come attitude for our lives. Happiness in either state is the attitude that opens up the greatest possibilities. Open and receptive.

To summarise this thought. Society is set up for us to earn good money in jobs that we have been trained for through the education that they supply. We then give it all away for stuff and to obediently create the lifestyle that they suggest. This produces the peaks and troughs in our lives and leaves us with continuous hope for something better or the thought that there must be something more and we will know what it is if we can just get more money and stuff. Easy Come - Easy Go.

Once we are aware of this we can choose not to give away our freedom totally and have faith that with the right middle attitude we can give off vibes that will attract money and all kinds of good into our lives. We just need to break the cycle of conformist enslavement. A look at one's life reveals quickly the repetitive behaviours and beliefs that keep us stuck in the cycle. With this in mind the following thoughts liberate us from the chains of money and will help us change to a new more realistic perspective that will better set us up for success. Success is purely and simply a state of mind becoming manifest throughout our lives. By changing our minds, we are changing our lives.

Life is a process of constant change. Money is no different and the flow must be continued with gratitude and love. Hoarding will never work it is regressive and life diminishing. Be grateful for your bills and the services provided. Pay bills with love and gratitude knowing that we are flowing as is the way of the Tao.

Beware of transmitting subtle messages of lack. This is easy to do when we have been taught to fear shortage of money and that very fear attracts the shortage that we fear. Fervently partaking in the lottery or gambling is a message that you are lacking and are not happy with your present situation.

Listen to your thoughts and self talk even in jest. Many a true word is spoken in jest. Suggestions of "never having enough" or "not being able to afford" are taken into the subconscious and become reality. This is why so many people get stuck where they are. These throw away thoughts and comments are repeatedly running our lives. Often disguised as jokes but in reality there are better forms of humour than deprecating comments. I should know I am the king of self-deprecation. My writing style has even been called self-deprecating, it was meant as a compliment but I am working on it. There is enough negativity to be fielded without our loading it up upon ourselves. This is why self-esteem is so important. We need to know we deserve whatever we desire in order to be open to receive. This is easier said than done and constant inner work is the order of the day for those not fortunate enough to be naturally this way inclined. The good news is that it is all doable and we can change whatever we damn well like about ourselves, that in itself is enough to empower us to more confidence and the desire to change.

By changing our communication with ourselves to a grateful optimistic interaction – "never having or being enough" is a suggestion we can do without. Once we begin to notice, it can be amazing how often we suggest things that do not serve us well. We are more negative as a default setting thanks to our conditioning and the constant bombardment with bad news and fear inducing stories. We are also led to believe that the ideals we are shown are what we should be. No surprise we do not feel good enough. Our intention must be to become positive as default and to see the crap we are bombarded with as exactly what it is. Rubbish. Constant repetition and correction works. If you are able to use a hypnotherapist to help and learn self-hypnosis (or teach yourself) you are able to re-programme your mind quickly and efficiently and life will change. It works, I witness it every day.

In keeping with the flow of money, give to charity. I buy the big issue to help the seller get back on his or her feet. It is their business. By helping them to succeed you will feel what it is like to open your own energy for success. That feeling is success. Success is a state of mind. Life flows. Keep it flowing. It doesn't hurt to talk to such people as this as they are positively acting to change their situation and listening can be motivational. Too often we are not ready to listen to others. And you will appreciate your own position that much more.  Tipping for services is good and paying a toll for the person behind or for a drink at the vending machine. These acts can really make the day for someone.  There are lots of ways to spread the feel good factor. Get imaginative. Why? The feeling you experience is your answer. Selfish, I know but giving feels good. And it is contagious. Imagine feeling that good all the time. Vibrating gratitude and love and primed for success.

Avoid getting into financial situations highlighting lack that are avoidable.  If we make things tight financially when we can avoid it, we are left with a constant nagging lack feeling. Keep a little in reserve even when you don't immediately need money.

Where possible get ahead with bills, groceries and anything that has caused concern previously. Learn from the past and encourage peace of mind at least with your financial situation. We can love money but only if we feel at harmony with it. Not if we fear it. Make it easy to be nonchalant about money. Phone calls chasing unpaid debts, bailiffs and empty food cupboards make it impossible to foster the attitude of plenty that we need to be pervasive in our lives.

Make whatever sacrifices are needed until a position of comfort can be reached and progress can be made from that point. Stop consuming luxuries no matter how you justify them until you reach that enviable position of plenty and buying the groceries you prefer as opposed to the cheapest (lack) of everything. The cheapest of everything is sending out that lack message.

In the past we have been in the situation of running out of food and being fearful of using the heating. These are not great situations when we are trying to create an abundance using our state of mind. The clash is obvious.

Lest you think I don't understand. There was decade in my life when we had so much debt that I was fearful of answering the phone or the front door because I was so often shocked by bailiffs or debt collectors chasing money that we didn't have or look likely to get anytime soon. Losing our business, cars and almost our relationship, not to mention our lives, was the state of our reality at that time. I have touched on this in my earlier books. It was a grim time and looking back now I see how we created our lives just as they were.

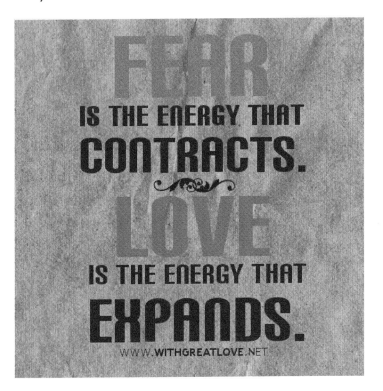

It is only the last few years that we have become very comfortable and have developed the attitude I am discussing here. I still fear the phone. I jump when it catches me off guard as does an unexpected knock at the door, but I am recovering. I am working on those habitual fears and these days knocks on the door are always good news and deliveries. We have zero debts or borrowing. Peace of mind is paramount. On the plus side this is why I am able to talk about this with so much authority on many of these common issues. And why I am such an effective self-help coach. I have made every mistake in the book of life and discovered workable real life solutions. All of these solutions are contained in our on-board computers. We just have to know how to use them. I wish I had met a me over a decade ago. But I probably wouldn't have listened. I have had to recover from having a real problem with money to one of relative prosperity. A life of totally lacking to one of comfort.

We now sit permanently in credit for our utilities and shop to ensure our cupboards are generously stacked with exactly what we want regardless of price. This creates a much healthier state of mind for giving and receiving. A position of personal power.

Whatever the opposite of value is, was what at that time money for us had turned into, the monster that was the root of all of our troubles. Or at least that is how it felt. One can imagine the fearful state of mind bought on by my previous situation. Living in fear, shame and lack and attributing it all to money. That is a lot of baggage for money to live with. Many of you have experienced similar and the far reaching effects this can have on the rest of one's life or the ability to progress away from that point.

Relationships, confidence, faith in life, will to live were all disappearing in a sea of helplessness and money was taking the rap. In hindsight it was all so avoidable by following the advice I am giving now and programming your mind for success, as we have done and continue to do each and every day. A job for life. We learned the hard way as human beings often have to. I hope I help at least some of you learn the easy way.

The secret to success is in the state of the mind. Whatever it takes to change the mind over to a programme of optimism and possibilities is what is needed. Begin with a genuine love, appreciation and respect for money that is neither fearful or obsessive. This is done by being comfortable, whatever it takes and removing all moments that are uncomfortable with regards to money, including suggesting with thought or words anything other than optimistically about your situation. That took us many years but we eventually got rid of all debt and climbed out of the hole of our own making.

Now after all of that when "I choose money now" it contains all of that work towards an eventual outcome of love and gratitude, optimism and freedom from the fear I had previously created. A wisdom based on knowledge through reading and study but crucially through experience and action. It is now a turbocharged fluid affirmation that will change and progress as I do.

I have or I have begun to open myself up to receive and my life reflects this in many ways that I didn't see coming but nevertheless serve me well. "My thoughts create my life" and "every day in every way I am getting better and better" are another two affirmations that have worked well and serve to fill my head with positive thoughts. Affirmations work in harmony with choosing to leave me open and receptive. But above all else, I no longer feel helpless or reliant on outside influences or luck. "I am always blessed with good luck". It is obvious in reading this that positive phrases become part of general language for those that use them. The opportunity to use them throughout day to day speaking and writing increases with practise. "I have all that I need to Succeed". We all do. And if you don't now just keep on saying and believing and you will rewrite that belief. For me my hypnotherapy has just quickened the process and helped me to understand my subconscious mind as one of two choices. Our subconscious can be either our greatest ally (soulmate) or our worst enemy as it was for me originally and still is the case for millions of people still suffering. It is worth keeping in mind when feeling at a low ebb that there are millions of people on this planet happy with much less than we have. Happy is a choice to be made. Make it every morning.

 **Choosing Health**

**Affirm - I choose vibrant health now.**

When I choose good health what meaning is contained in this simple sentence for me?

Here are some of the thoughts consciously or unconsciously present in my mind when this affirmation is spoken, read or written.

Knowing that vibrant health is a choice is my first core belief. It is quite a radical belief by normal conformist standards but that is what I believe.

Our hearts and minds are of primary importance when it comes to our physical health. Where are hearts and minds lead our material world lives follow. We operate as a unified whole not as a machine with bits and pieces to be fixed. Illness is the biggest business on the planet alongside weapons of mass destruction. It is therefore important not to get caught in the net of illness by bringing it into our focus at every opportunity or by letting ourselves be invaded by thoughts of disease. If we suggest illness to ourselves or others we are very often right. "I always catch" or "If it's going around I will catch it" are affirmations guaranteed to come true. Henry Ford had a saying – "Whether you think you can or you think you can't, you will be right." That applies across the board. Our minds are powerful and we get what we think about all day. Thoughts about illness are even turbocharged with strong emotions making them potent attracting thoughts.

Watching advertisements for illness cures and charities on any media can be argued to foster thoughts leading to contracting what is being to all intents and purposes advertised to the unsuspecting viewers. This is deliberate. Billions are sold the idea of flu each year and then sold the cure. Remember thoughts become things. Guard yours.

It is high time we wised up and began to protect ourselves from the damaging memes or thought viruses that we are exposed to by the hidden rulers who care little whether we live or die as long as there is something in it for them. Toxic people, thoughts, ads etc. as memes kill just as surely as bullets but much more subtly and mostly undetected. By all means help the sick and charities but don't expose yourself to the constant fear inducing sales pitches that create illness in any of us exposed for long enough to take the suggestions deep into our unconscious minds.

> Don't let negative and toxic people rent space in your head. Raise the rent and kick them out!
>
> – Robert Tew

Repetitive trance tactics are used to control and enslave. With this book we can use the same methods to free ourselves with affirmations and chosen thoughts. As you read recollect how pharma companies list symptoms in ads the same way I would if I were using hypnosis to give you the flu. These ads are repeated throughout your life on various mediums, soaking into your subconscious. This is just one illness. Start to see all advertising as aimed at changing your behaviour, making you dissatisfied or ill, whatever it takes for either profit or power. My grandson's first coherent sentence was "out now on dvd". We are being programmed as consumers for life. Illness means we have to consume. We can begin to defend against this crap but we have to get rid of the crap from our lives. Re-programme our own minds for success. We can be who we chose to be not who we are expected to be for others profit and control. I am sorry to harp on but this is so important and we can all act on this in our lives.

In summary of this point understanding our minds in relation to our health as not being separate entities. The enemies of this process exploit our ignorance of our own minds. Awareness of this simple truth unlocks the door to our freedom, amazing possibilities, perfect bodies and vibrant health. By keeping illness as much as possible out of our realities we take the first step to perfect health.

Our bodies can regenerate and recover, it can even be argued that there is no reason why we age other than a collective and personal belief in the aging process programmed into us all and reinforced constantly via the various mediums. How often is age discussed? A disproportionate amount.

It has been argued that theoretically illness can be eliminated for the human race and that it suits certain powers to retain sickness and suffering as a form of fear induced control and distraction. Are there already cures for cancer. Would it cost the pharma giants if there were? Which is more profitable and fear inducing? Do we look in the wrong place for cures when we are ill?

We can heal ourselves and others.

We all know the person that affirms "I never get ill" or "I don't have time for illness" and that suggestion combined with the total indifference to illness becomes imprinted in the unconscious mind and the reality is exactly that. Thoughts are things. Powerful energy. Energy is what the universe is made of. It is not so hard to believe that what we think we know is wrong. This person has aligned their words with that deep unconscious expectation and that is their life. They are an exception to the current beliefs. We are all exceptions to current beliefs. A new way of thinking is coming.

Another example is "I can eat whatever I like and I never gain weight" – The unconscious great expectation is the same and once again we have an individual human being that contradicts the current science. But there is no profit in naturally lean people. These are all affirmations that we all need to adopt. Seriously, no matter how far away we are from that now we must begin to expect that we can think our way to a perfectly healthy life whilst defending ourselves from others that profit from the opposite and our suffering.

Please! If you take one thing from this book let it be how your mind works and its limitless power to produce what we are conditioned to believe are miracles but in reality each and every one of us is equipped with these basic human "talents". Talents that we have been programmed to forget or that are new to us as a rapidly evolving species. If we can unlearn everything we are programmed to believe we will find the truth for us is very different. Great expectations are just the start. The power of suggestion is a genuine force that is used to control us by the dark side. We can use the same to regain our lives and save this planet and mankind. Note the similarity to the Star Wars mythology in the truth. That is why we are drawn to myths they hold more truth than the accepted truths and have done throughout the ages. Look to man's greatest myths for your answers. Many of us do already but spoil it by believing that they are literal and historical accounts. They are not and lose much when interpreted in that way.

When I choose health. I choose something that I have control over and I am empowered to choose my own health.

 ## Choosing Body

**Affirm - I choose my body now.**

By now you should be feeling pretty empowered and know that it is your own mind that can set you free and just because you can't see it as you can your body it is nevertheless crucial to your life. BodyMind. Always a team.

Visualise. See, feel, hear, use your senses with your imagination to see your perfect body from every angle. Naked and clothed, as you wish it to be, expect it. Watch it move, feel it move, dance, play, laugh and feel how you feel emotionally in this your newly ordered body. This is your body. If this can be done in a trance state, all the better. Extreme relaxation is how trance feels. Attach one or more affirmations to this "body movie", use the short affirmation to ignite your movie. I choose my body is good. When this becomes your unconscious expectation your miracle will happen. Believe in yourself. Love yourself.

**Julie (Grandmother) at 53. Me (57)**

Using your imagination and thoughts to create your life and in this case your body is being used already by cultural forces constantly via norms and ideals. Now you will learn to do it for yourself. You have the body you have created. And you can change that when you are prepared to do the work. Induce a trance state and watch your body on a screen in your mind's eye. Head to toe from every angle. See the muscle move, watch as you exercise. Do house work, dance, interact with others and even make love. You choose,

It's your imagination, your choice. Your imagination is your only limitation, you must believe it, feel it and know that it is not only possible but that it has already begun. You have nothing to lose. Faith in your mind's ability to operate your life is paramount. Use these affirmations regularly in addition to specific ones. There are no situations that these two will not help.

**My positive thoughts create my life.**

**I release all self-doubt and negativity.**

Just before you go to sleep and just after you wake up are good times to watch the movie. And don't forget to let go of it now and again with an indifference born from knowing that it is done. Events in your life will begin to shift to suit your new creation

 **Choosing Super fitness**

**Affirm - I choose super fitness now.**

As with everything fitness begins with a thought – superfitness is a state of made visible to the senses. Superfitness can be visualised along with our perfect bodies and our vibrant health. All of our choices will eventually harmonise to move us towards wholeness. There is no separation only oneness in our visible and invisible world. We are everything. Our fitness is a result of our mind primarily, with our health and body and next we will look at nutrition which again connects perfectly. The same will be true throughout this book and your life. Everything is connected, nothing is separate.

To begin when we discuss or think about our fitness we are always superfit, we visualise the finished creation as if it is already a done deal. When we choose superfitness this is the image that we are creating. A simple affirmation begins our on-board programming which we are writing on our subconscious with our thoughts, words, feelings and images via our mental movies. We will never put ourselves down or allow others to put us down or be anything less than superfit. Remembering that our suggestion will shift events to become conducive to our new reality. We will begin to find new behaviours easy to adopt and the universe changing to meet our needs. We are superfit now. We see only superfitness. At the gym, walking, dancing, doing housework.

We love activity. We like to exercise our whole body in all kinds of ways. Our heart loves that we exercise. We love to move in any way shape or form. Our bodies are perfect for moving. We feel good

160

when we move. We like to play at any stage of life. When we imagine and play our mental movie we see a fit healthy body in action of all sorts. We feel it, see it vividly and even hear compliments and small talk. Maybe even playing music and singing while we move with energy and vitality. Sex is always fun to imagine for a fit healthy body. Watch your fit healthy body live the life you are creating. Watch the posture and confidence as you exercise and move in various activities. Maybe even learn a new skill in your movie such as riding a bike, ice skating or any of the myriad of physical skills on offer for the energetic these days. I know one young man that could not swim or ride a bike, he used this opportunity to learn both by supplementing his visualisation with physical practice he succeeded where he had previously failed. He was able to make his impossible possible by first becoming an expert in his mind and then physically. He no longer has to avoid either pursuit due to embarrassment. Initially all of his visualisation was performed under hypnosis and loosely scripted by me. Eventually he was able to use self-hypnosis and trance states alone and in many other areas of his life including learning to drive with the occasional guidance and encouragement from me. He is now totally self-reliant and fully realises the power of his mind. He is progressing nicely through the life he is now creating. The more the practice the greater the mastery. Fitness is a state of mind every day and in each moment. It is moving and embracing life. It is walking, biking and dancing. You don't have to join a gym, just get up and go. It is that simple. Get off your arse. Fitness is the opposite of lazy. Our tech makes us lazy. Get up and go as a way to balance the books. Move more – eat less. When you choose to affirm superfitness we want mind boggling value to emerge.

**Choosing Nutrition**

**Affirm - I choose positive nutrition now.**

What expectations do we need to programme into our minds in order for our nutrition to enhance our lives?

We can see clearly now that each element of our choosing compliments the whole. This is where the term holistic hypnotherapy arises in my practise. Hypnotherapy sessions and trance moments are all focused on the big picture of our progress across the choices that we value and the values that we choose. Harmonising the values is the natural way our mind works. When I scrip or freestyle the sessions with my partners it is with the view of total progress. I often use scripts covering such values as good health, motivation, success and love all in the same single session. Each being intrinsically linked to the other and ultimately to total self-improvement. I coach my partners to do the same with their self-hypnosis, visualisation and relaxation sessions. It is far more natural to imagine the big picture than to attempt to isolate certain aspects and create separation. Here are some of the points that I have integrated into what choosing nutrition means to me. However, choosing is a fluid process and as new positive aspects enter the equation the process evolves.

First thing that springs to mind is that when using the body actively and intensely with exercise that balanced feeds are important, including all of the essentials for recovery and energy requirements. My book handy *Feeding The Active Body by Gary Walsh* will help a great deal with what the requirements might be and give lots of

162

alternatives and pointers for what and when to eat. It can be ordered from Amazon for a reasonable price. I also have the colossal Great Body Bible available by The Fitness Wizards. A 700+ page personal trainer for your coffee table should you need to get deep into health and fitness.

I am mindful that living in the land of plenty as we all do, normal eating is generally over-eating and that a policy of less is more is a wise mantra. This means less bulk consumed but maximum nutritional content. I have learned my body runs best relatively empty and that include my brain and thinking process. Fullness is never an intended or ideal condition for a person with ready access to good food. Eating small amounts of nutrition rich food is the wise choice.

Fasting is good, I fast often for anything from 18 hours to 60 hours and have only ever had good results in my physique and fitness. It feels good and the empty feeling can be very comfortably once transformed into a positive in one's mind. Once I cast off the programming that I have been bombarded with since birth that more is better, the empty, tight feeling becomes very positive and an indicator of results and an affirmation of my self-discipline. My energy is always good.

I exercise most days and I always walk the hills with the dogs at first light. I always go to the gym on an empty stomach after walking the dogs, 5.30am at this time of year. In an average days eating I include the following –

- A small protein shake after gym with skimmed milk, eggs and a banana.
- Oatmeal made with skimmed milk and some protein powder

- A tuna roll and fruit.
- High protein soft cheese (similar to yoghurt) with added nut and seeds.
- A large bowl of mixed salad and raw veg and another small protein shake.
- I may have a glass of milk at the end of the day but more often than not I try to stop feeding as early as possible to lengthen the time fasting between my last feed and first feed the next day. Sometimes I fast intermittently like this for 18 hours each day for weeks on end. My eating all happens in 6 hours after the gym session in the morning.
- Variations on this plan always work well for me and it is important that I believe that. Believe in your eating plan and you will achieve great results.

Affirmations along these lines will work well – *I love raw veg – I love feeling empty – Less food makes me feel very good – less is more*. Remember when you affirm that you focus on the positive not on the negative of any problem foods as your subconscious doesn't know the difference. Affirm the way you would like to eat and how you know you will get to where you are headed. I now eat foods that I used to turn my nose up to by affirming the positive. It really is that simple. The image shown of my abs at 57 years old was taken whilst on this type of plan. Another good affirmation is I *always have a six pack.* I say this whether I have one or not and I firmly believe that it will be a reality, it normally is. My diet is okay, but I am sure that my attitude and expectations have more to do with my body than any perfect eating habits. I expect to be in shape and I enjoy exercise.

**Me (57).**

I constantly battle as many of us do with an attachment to food built up over many years of brainwashing. The advantage I have is that I now know that it is a battle and that gives me back my freedom. It has been a struggle but I now see how we are all led to this attachment by a society that places profit before people. I now eat to live; I no longer live to eat or by association to television or being bored. My first few fasts helped me ease this attachment and the realisation that our minds are the key and whoever owns the mind is in control of their actions fully. I still feel the pull of the conditioning and attachments waiting in the wings. I am in control. I buy the food. I am free to choose.

I am aware that sweet, fatty and strong tasting foods spoil my taste for natural flavours. My bowl of raw veg has become a real pleasure from beginning as a relatively tasteless chore. I am wise to the purveyors of crap and their ploy to have us brainwashed and addicted to their shite masquerading as nutrition. If we want a high performance body, we need high performance foods. Simple!

I view adhering to good nutrition habits as a real genuine success in our "eat shit and die" society. Excuse the phrase but I think we pussy foot around these issues too much and fail to realise the gravity or seriousness of them on our health and longevity. Success begets success, it is motivating to know I am at least aware of my nemesis and have a semblance of control.

Everything we understand about food could be wrong! It pays to be very cynical when the latest fads and trends appear. Be independent, the basics rarely change. Decide your stance and look after yourself. Monitor your moods and feelings after food and adjust accordingly. Know exactly what you mean when you affirm that "I choose positive nutrition now". Buy my book, it is low cost and it is a good guide to the basics for feeding the active body. Remember when it comes to nutrition if something seems to god to be true it probably is and that includes the latest diet. If they all worked so well, we would never need them after the first good one. Eat smart. Be positive.

Speak of only good nutritional habits even if you deviate from your intended plan. Auto-suggestion is powerful – use it constantly. Talk the perfect nutritional plan and it will become your reality. Never beat yourself up about moments of weakness. Accept your shadow lesson and continue on your zig zag road to success. Continue to release all negativity and use your mind to create your life. Good nutrition begins with a single thought.

For decades I was telling myself and others "I don't like veg" (suggestion) – then I discovered the power of the mind and it turns out I can like veg just fine and had developed a negative attitude through my childhood experiences. I simply suggested that veg is fine and I faked it until I like veg now. The old belief has been overwritten.

When "I choose positive nutrition" all of this and more is contained within that very small value sentence. When we choose positive nutrition we choose good habits and a positive relationship to the food we eat and the feelings that it brings to our whole being. If this is not true, then we can choose to change to such a relationship. It does help to defend against the constant brainwashing for unhealthy foods via the media and others. How you do that is up to you but it will make your life easier if you do something positive to delete the negative influences from your life.

 **Choosing Motivation**

**Affirm – I choose Motivation now**

When we choose motivation it is wise to be aware that we will experience periods of demotivation as a normal occurrence. The aim is to notice and accept those periods as part of the process of growth and minimise any negative impact they may have. Such moments should be viewed as springboards to success. Without the opposite to motivation we would have no motivation. Light is only light as compared to dark. The same for motivation (light) and demotivation (dark).

When we choose motivation what value does the word contain?

In motivating ourselves we use other values that harmonise to produce motivation.

Gratitude – We take a good long look at all of the blessings in our lives. This motivates us.

Success – We reflect on our successes and what success may mean to us and in which areas of our lives we are successful. This motivates us.

Optimism – We learn to be more optimistic. Optimism can be learned. **Martin Seligman's book Learned Optimism** can help with this. Optimism is motivating.

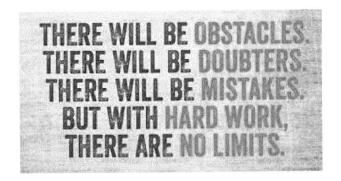

THERE WILL BE OBSTACLES. THERE WILL BE DOUBTERS. THERE WILL BE MISTAKES. BUT WITH HARD WORK, THERE ARE NO LIMITS.

Motivation is also about harnessing and transforming our energies, many of those energies often being used negatively. We have lots of energy I our bodies and surrounding us with names such as prana – life energy – chi – libido – Eros and many more terms, too many to mention. We are veritable balls of energy. Directing this energy is a skill worth learning. Anger is an example of an emotion loaded with energy that could benefit from some redirection. Anger can be accepted and transformed, not played out or repressed. Never feeling fear, anger or stress would be a worry and a recipe for an explosion of negative energy (rage) but recognising as natural and transforming the energy in the above states is where the real can be found. This requires being aware of the feelings and working with the energy in a positive and transforming way, and before we lose control of ourselves altogether. The act of transforming negative energy is in itself motivating, even simply knowing that we can change motivates us, particularly if we have felt at the mercy of our emotions previously. Remember those very wise words from Henry Ford – "Whether you think you can or you think you can't you'll be right". I use another affirmation – "I can and I will" when feeling a little doubtful. What you think matters to what happens in your life.

An example of this transformation process in action is that moment when we are fuming and something triggers us to laugh or more accurately to giggle like school children. Our pride wants to stay mad but we are powerless to fight the urge to giggle. We all need to giggle like school children more often. What an awesome way to use energy. A great sense of humour is priceless. Laughter is a great device for transforming negative energy. It does also help to hold in your mind some visions that can be called upon to begin the transformation from negative to positive. A funny scene or a loving moment, whatever it takes to shift the energy in a more positive direction. I suppose you could even carry a picture but we can take the best still pictures with our minds and carry them with us. At the moment I have my grandchildren playing, my pups being mischievous and Julie laughing at me falling over as quick mood changers. I am even smiling and laughing typing this section. It works. The key is that no matter how right we think we are, anger serves nobody, least of all ourselves. Giggling is a fine example of how simply choosing to be better does work. It is far better to be kind to others and ourselves than to be right. Loving both ourselves and others is the key to this kindness. Starting with ourselves. If we tend to need an aggressive outlet, then exercise is a fantastic way to transform negative energy towards positive ends. I note here how rugby and boxing two violent sports display the gentlest of human beings (Manny Pacquiao) off the field of play once the energy has been transformed. Any loving couple will have experienced how anger can be transformed into passion and the resulting sex is awesome. Angry sex does take some beating as a way for two consenting lovers to transform angry negative energy. Don't deny your shadow, work with it and progress in every way.

When choosing motivation all of this is contained within the choice, within one small sentence, together with associated images, sounds, feelings and emotions. Now choosing motivation is truly a turbo charged choice for me to make. Packed with positive energy whilst acknowledging my shadow side. The most powerful motivating force for humanity is love – by transforming anger we have energised love for self and others. Powerful motivation.

I went through a period in my life when I had little or no control over my rage. Or so I believed and that became my reality at that time. The damage was contained and realised and I have used exactly these methods to conquer my demons. There is a key moment (a tipping point) in all situations and I learned how to win that moment with love – breathing and walking away and with perseverance the rages stopped entirely with an acceptance that nothing is worth the pain and suffering caused. I had a choice. I just surrendered. I let go of struggle. Nowadays I just get pissed off a tad like other people and shrug it off. More importantly my life transformed from the moment I chose to stop being angry. I consider myself lucky to get the opportunity to learn and grow and something sticks in my mind to this day. A person I love more than life itself looking exasperated and full of love just saying to me "Adam! You are always so angry these days". Simply put, but she was so right. I can see her helpless look in my mind now. I decided at that moment that life could never be good if I spent it permanently angry and full of blame with life itself and at that moment I chose differently. I decided that I was making it impossible for her to love me and I had to learn to love myself to make it change. I changed the way I thought. That was all I could change, I can't change anything else. And it worked. The outside changed when I changed the inside. From that moment all of that energy I had wasted on anger and blame rerouted into motivation and it has been that way ever since. I have gone from a man wanting to end his life ASAP after three of my friends chose exactly that route, to a man that wants to squeeze every last drop from my time in the mortal realm. Just by changing my mind and thoughts. I would say I still have moments of doubt but now I know that I get to choose and I am able to deal with anything that comes along. My past still occasionally pokes me in the ribs and I have to let it go. I let all of my yesterday's go each and every day.

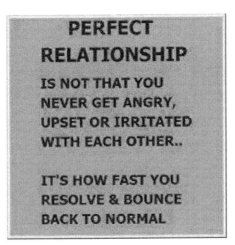

PERFECT RELATIONSHIP IS NOT THAT YOU NEVER GET ANGRY, UPSET OR IRRITATED WITH EACH OTHER..

IT'S HOW FAST YOU RESOLVE & BOUNCE BACK TO NORMAL

It is my firm belief that my capacity for rage developed from years of turning the other cheek and being "good" as instructed by my parents. A gentle giant. Nowadays I work with my shadow side to create balance, I no longer see it as a choice of good over its opposite. I merely accept and control both aspects of my psyche on a psychological level. I balance my light and dark in the knowledge that without the other neither can exist. If you want to be the best you can be. Acknowledge the worst you can be and fuse them into one. Chilled demons and cheeky heroes.

The sub title of my books was originally "Finding meaning in midlife". I changed it to "Finding motivation in midlife" because I see so many people going through the motions of a life that they feel has finished all apart from the last bit. Meaning is just one way to motivation. Success, fitness, money, love etc. etc. there are so many other ways to stay motivated in life and all equally valid. If we can live a life that motivates us to live it well, that is perfect. Wherever that motivation comes from. I will deal with success in the next section.

##  Choosing Success

**Affirm – I choose success**

When choosing success, what value can we build into that word to motivate us to even greater success? There is no reason that we can't become more successful throughout life. And in areas that we have never before considered.

> ## SUCCESS
>
> *To laugh often and much; to win the respect of intelligent people and the affection of children; to earn the appreciation of honest critics and endure the betrayal of false friends; to appreciate beauty, to find the best in others; to leave the world a bit better, whether by a healthy child, a garden patch or a redeemed social condition; to know even one life has breathed easier because you have lived. This is to have succeeded.*
>
> —*Ralph Waldo Emerson*

Success can mean different things to different people particularly when we shed the belief that success means having the biggest pile of stuff possible when we end our lives. Often it is the small things that we will be remembered for and the small things that will have the biggest impact on others. Think about somebody that you consider successful in their lives. Are they too busy amassing stuff to enjoy life or are they balanced throughout their lives? Often we get caught up in the more is better lifestyle in the first part of our lives but thankfully we have the opportunity to concentrate on what is really important as we reach midlife. Our motivation often changes and we wake up.

I am striving for success in areas that I would never have considered early in my life and some that I have always thought important but for different reasons. When I choose to affirm success these are some of the areas that I am currently valuing. My goals change and with them my definition of success at any given moment.

One area that has always featured for me is my health and fitness, but I used to train to mould a body acceptable both to myself and others and if I am honest what others thought was the deal clincher for my own self-worth. There are remnants of this left behind but nowadays I train and care for my body for myself and because I consider my body a precious gift that should be respected and I have a vision for my body for myself that may fit others expectations but that is no longer my driving motivation. I am not so obsessive and do not work-out as much to change the shape of my body as much as I like to get out and about in nature, biking and walking. I still feel intense progressive resistance exercise for the whole body is vital as it is weight bearing and the health benefits as we age are priceless. The look of my body is now a by-product of my fitness regime as opposed to being the sole focus as it once was. It is nice to be in control of myself and not at the mercy of external forces when it comes to the condition of one of my greatest gifts. As for nutrition I am now aware what makes me feel good and what doesn't and that is why I eat healthy foods. I also allow myself to eat forbidden foods without guilt and that results in a more relaxed approach to food and a better all around diet. It's that simple. Success in health and fitness is gauged by how I feel, my energy levels and how I look, aiming for low body-fat levels and good muscle tone. They are measurements for health and fitness success. If I find myself becoming too intense I just shrug and back off.

Listening more and talking less is another current goal and one that I have been working on to change my brains hardwiring for quite some time. I am progressing and do not have so many getting carried away moments when I chat to others. I actually enjoy listening and no longer think what I have to say is the most important thing in the world and the world will end without my valuable input. My gauge for success here is Julie. I just ask her to honestly monitor my progress. But to be honest it is obvious when I am "on it" because the feeling is one of calm and being present as opposed to being out of control. Also when that urge for the words to fall out arises I am abler to let it go by without yapping.

Linked in with this goal is the goal of treating the person I am with at any moment as the most important in my life and the moment as the most important moment. This is in line with Buddhist thinking that no other moments exist apart from the present moment. This is

improving but it can take me a long time to get home from a walk if there are a lot of people to meet.

THE PAST IS GONE, THE FUTURE IS NOT YET HERE, AND IF WE DO NOT GO BACK TO OURSELVES *IN THE PRESENT* MOMENT, WE CANNOT BE IN *TOUCH* WITH LIFE.

— THICH NHAT HANH

I also see the behaviour of my three dogs as a success on any given day as they react to who I am inside, their senses finely tuned to mine. If I am having issue with them I look inside of myself for the answers. Three canine teachers. When we are in harmony all is well.

I am being more mindful of my thoughts. Success measured by having less toxic thoughts or at least catching them and dealing with them before they rule my life.

I am reducing my food portions across the board in order to manage my weight.

The health of the plant life in my world is also a measure of success for me. I consider my plants a direct link to my energy levels. If I am loving they flourish, if I am less than loving they will struggle.

For me these are just a few current goals that when I affirm success I visualise. I see them as a done deal, perfectly successful now. That is what I expect and that is generally what I get. There are times when I feature more materialistic goals but I have found that if I change myself as much as possible my material world is okay.

As an example. I damaged the engine of Hermes my Dodge Nitro through negligence. I visualise Hermes back and perfect in my life. Safe, reliable, secure and beautiful. Hermes is one of my animated objects. Full of character and life for me and Julie. I don't use a car much at all, often weeks go by while we use our bikes to get around but then we have a need motorised transport and when I do I like a personality. Hermes is that. I have him covered in quotes and signs. He is beautiful and part of the clan.

Hermes is unique, unpredictable and totally suitable for us. They don't make Dodge Nitros anymore, many would say with good reason but for me he is just perfect. For me the law of attraction works if I don't try to change my life radically. It has to be believable for my subconscious expectations and I need to be generally positive and that is what I now work on. I try to think about what I want more than what I don't want. We all have the habit of thinking about the stuff we don't want in our lives, encouraged by the media. The wars against cancer, drugs and terrorism focus on what we do not want and as such all of those situations are getting worse. That is the law of attraction in action. Changing myself to think about the life that I want is my aim and I am improving. Getting better is not all about lots of stuff. It is more about finding some peace of mind and leading an interesting life.

### Friedrich Nietzsche

Fellow man! Your whole life, like a sandglass, will always be reversed and will ever run out again, - a long minute of time will elapse until all those conditions out of which you were evolved return in the wheel of the cosmic process. And then you will find every pain and every pleasure, every friend and every enemy, every hope and every error, every blade of grass and every ray of sunshine once more, and the whole fabric of things which make up you in which you are but a grain.

Nietzsche thought that if we would live our lives as they are over and over again quite happily forever then we are leading a good life. I am not sure about that yet but I am at the stage where I would not be terribly disappointed or feel that it was a torturous existence. And I do feel it just gets better. That is progress for me. There have been times when any life at all was the choice for me. How times have changed.

Last but not least for many is success in our material worlds measured by stuff and money. We can see in our minds eye our chosen material world. We can tell a different story about our home, car and possessions in as much detail as our imaginations will allow and with exercise our imaginations will get better and stronger. This is where ideas for tools such as a dream board arise featuring all that we wish to create in our lives. Creative visualisation techniques are great for this as you live the life you are creating as you create it. Story telling sessions are also a good way to expand our vision of how we see our lives developing. These images stay with us and grow as our imagination flexes its muscles. A skill that may have lain dormant since childhood. Or worse is only used to imagine the worst as encouraged by the media and social control mechanisms. For many of us our days are spent in fear of what may happen in this world that is going ruin. I have a feeling that the world is in much better shape than is depicted on the television and news and that while we are focused on attracting what we don't want we are missing out on what we do want. How much of the worlds turbulence is created by the reverse law of attraction? Our thoughts attracting what we don't want just as they do for what we do want.

Now that we have looked at affirmations and how the words thoughts and feelings can direct our lives and how we can increase the value of the words and thoughts that we choose, I will discuss a few of the ways that we use them in rituals that I feel maximise their benefits over time and help reinforce the new habits. Originally we dedicated a day to choosing and took every opportunity throughout that day to overwrite negative thoughts by choosing our own values. We named it -

 **I Choose Tuesday**

Quite simply we would repeatedly choose values over and over either in our minds or out loud if we were in the position to do so. We would also write them out. Below are a sample of the choices. I found that a grim mood when out walking could be transformed very quickly to one of optimism. Remembering we can only think about one thing at a time explains this very well. I always felt resistance from Mr Grumpy and even struggled to think of anything to choose as grumpiness ruled but once I focused and learned to ignore that and persevere Mr Grumpy transformed to Mr Happy in double quick time.

I choose nature today

I choose magic today

I choose smiles today

I choose kindness today

I choose patience today

I choose tolerance today

I choose forgiveness today

I choose gratitude today

I choose faith today

I choose fun today

I choose surrender today

I choose safety and security now

I choose intuition today

I choose calm now

I choose divine guidance today

I choose to be receptive today

I choose acceptance now

I choose faith now

I choose to let go now

I choose to hand it over now

And the list goes on. I have note books loaded with affirmed choices that all serve me better than my negative chatter box ever did or does. There are no rules and I found that whatever I felt that I needed on the day seemed to just pop into my head as I trusted the process and that is vital – To trust the process. The mere act of linking together choices one after the other is great for focusing the mind away from any petty trivialities that may be occupying he mind negatively. I would keep going for a long while and even repeat the choices that felt particularly good and struck a chord on a deeper level. I use it often to fall asleep to. Choosing good thoughts before you sleep is a perfect way to end the day.

We even had the other days set out for focused behaviours. Surrender Saturday – Funday Sunday – Wake up Wednesday – Forgiveness Friday – Gratitude Monday and Faith Thursday. All serving the purpose of focusing our attention on any given day. We still use Forgiveness Friday and Gratitude Monday occasionally but more often both are included in our daily thinking as normal. The purpose was always to create normal behaviours around the daily focus. You can invent your own days if you feel any of the above needs more work and will benefit from a more intense period of practise.

### A new Life Every Day

We watch the sunrise from the top of the hills close to our home each day. We have turned this into a rewarding ritual.

We put together a fire in a box. We have wind proof lighters and I use a small box stuffed with papers and firelighters. We both have a desk calendar, a Dilbert one currently and rip off the day before each day after making notes about what we are grateful for and any negativity that we may need to let go of. So we have a small list of both from the day before. We have some favourite places for our ritual and once we get settled and the fire is alight we both say a few words of gratitude and burn our page a day offerings. This ritual is our way of giving thanks and letting go of the past and beginning a new life each day. There are times when the sunrises are breathtakingly spectacular and the all-important feelings are very good. We have developed a little saying to further enhance the moment.

**"Ashes to ashes dust to dust letting yesterday go as we know we must.**

**Ashes to ashes dust to dust surrendering now as in God's(Tao's) grace we trust."**

We began by doing this just on full and new moons but it is so enjoyable that we do it as often as we can. It is a fantastic way to set oneself up for the new day. Choosing a new life every day. Many think fire is a destructive force but we see it as transforming energy into a more dynamic form fit to mingle with the universe. Energy cannot be destroyed. It my firm belief that ritual transforms human psychic energies and is a lost art. The new rituals of television and smartphones are no substitute. And you not what else? RITUALS ARE FUN!

# *An early-morning* walk is a *blessing* for the whole day.

- Henry David Thoreau

**Storytime**

The stories we tell ourselves are what create our lives and that fact is one of the main reasons that we create as much awe and wonder in our lives as possible.  Even for the most optimistic of us our conditioned to be limited stories based often on our past mistakes are not going to create very good lives. More often repeating all of the same stuff in a cycle of habit believing that is just the way we are and we have no choice. We need to at least create our perfect worlds in our thoughts and make them as real as possible. Which is why they need to be achievable to that logical part of you that is still limited. Small steps will get you wherever you want to go. Our story telling time is open and we can help the other with the stories and add if we wish. As both Julie and I want the same or to share much of the same life it helps if we can see it the same way. An example of the stories could be one where we enter our dream house and have a shower or cook a meal in the perfect bathroom or kitchen. Details that mean something to either are easy to insert and fun. Driving your dream car on a date together is another idea. Training your bodies together and eating a post workout meal is another good story line. Being as descriptive and humorous as possible is good and we have improved over the brief time that we have been doing this. The imagination is the only limit, however I really do think that it seeming possible to your logical side does help cut down resistance from your subconscious fears and limited beliefs. I would say really stretch your possibilities and you will be about right. So for instance if you love nothing better than a hot, powerful shower that invigorates your whole being and you have less than that and you love a massive comfortable bed but yours is limited by where you are. You then tell the story of the house of your dreams including an amazing shower experience that you can feel and a bed that once again you can describe and experience in your mind. None of that is beyond belief for even the most limited of us. What you expect will expand once you have experienced a few miracles for yourself. Write the stories down as often our lives change and we forget we have created them until we find the evidence of our writing. I recently found this piece of writing and whilst it was not what I meant when I wrote it, it does accurately describe our home now.

> *"A beautiful new home, close to nature, for the pups, plants and humans. Comfortable, warm and perfect for our lifestyle. A home that dreams are made of, surrounded by love and bathed in the wonders of the universe. A home that creates perfect peace of mind and a place where creativity and love abound. A home that welcomes all with a feeling of being so right. A place of serenity and calmness. A home to grow spiritually with others."*

I had scribbled this on a piece of scrap cardboard and was using it as a book mark. It dropped out the other day and I realised that could describe our home now. You will notice that there is not one material request for money or more stuff, but rather those invisible treasures that we try to find through having more stuff. I subsequently rewrote it to factor in our new starting point, this time being more specific and to progress us to another beautiful home whilst being very grateful for where we are now.

Storytime is a fun guided visualisation that includes anyone that may be part of your life. Life, all said and done is about cooperation and if you are living with person your vision should be aligned and I believe that is the best use of the energies. Loving fun energy has to be the most effective, doesn't it?

 **The right side of the bed**

The right ritual in the morning while you are still between wake and sleep is crucial to your follow through mood for the day. Start right keep it going.

I wake up and sit on the edge of the bed. I say thanks three times and then I say something like "Today something amazingly smashing is going to happen to each of us." Or "The spirit of the Tao showers us with unexpected blessings constantly." I say us to keep the theme of power in loving numbers going. Julie and I have worked long and hard to be a loving team and that is the way we will progress. Julie does similar.

> "Watch your thoughts; they become words. Watch your words; they become actions. Watch your actions; they become habits. Watch your habits; they become character. Watch your character; it becomes your destiny." – Lao-Tze –

I then put on my onesie (don't laugh) and with music player in my pocket I play myself happy tunes until I have made my tea and jigged about in the kitchen. I use binaural beats and affirmations for 40 minutes after that to further set myself up for success. I love the peace and quiet of that time in the morning and at times I just sit listening to the beating clock and affirm to that rhythm as it produces a very similar brain state. The peace of mind I feel after my morning moments are priceless. I feed the pups, make some tea and wake Julie after. I get up an hour before Julie and it is always at least an hour before sunrise as we aim for the hills by sunrise. Julie has a slightly different routine but includes similar practices. Happy or grumpy is a choice that we can all make. I have always been on the serious side about life. For too many years I settled for grumpy as I felt I had no choice. We all have a choice.

You can contact me if you want to know what tunes I play at - adamsenex@virginmedia.com or register on my site and mail me from there www.adamsenex.com.

189

## Conclusion

One of the tunes that I use in my wake up period is Crazy by Seal.

### *Crazy*

*In a church by her face*
*he talks about the people going under*

*Only child know*

*A man decides after seventy years*
*That what he goes there for, is to unlock the door*
*While those around him criticize and sleep*
*And through a fractal on a breaking wall*
*I see you my friend, and touch your face again*
*Miracles will happen as we trip*

*But we're never gonna survive, unless*
*We get a little crazy*
*No we're never gonna survive, unless*
*We are a little crazy*

*In a sky full of people, only some want to fly*
*Isn't that crazy*
*In a world full of people, only some want to fly*
*Isn't that crazy, crazy*
*In a heaven of people there's only some want to fly*
*Ain't that crazy*
*Oh babe, oh darlin'*
*In a world full of people there's only some want to fly*
*Isn't that crazy, isn't that crazy, isn't that crazy, isn't that*
*crazy*

*But were never gonna survive unless, we get a little crazy*
*No were never gonna to survive unless we are a little*
*But were never gonna survive unless, we get a little crazy*
*No were never gonna to survive unless, we are a little, crazy*
*No no, never survive unless, we get a little bit*

190

*And then you see things*
*The size of which you've never known before*

*They'll break it*

*Someday, only child know*

*Them things*
*The size of which you've never known before*

*Someday, someway, someway, someway, someday, someday*

That could be the mantra that saves the human race. Currently, any person straying from the considered norms is considered crazy or at least a little weird. Consider this! The norms are currently plunging the planet and the human race into a situation in which the end will be predictable and messy.  The norms are plainly not working. Suffering and misery is the legacy that our current norms will leave for us. "I am not crazy; I am just not you." This is as another book title about personality types that describes our reaction to anybody being different from us. Most of the wars on this planet are because others are different in some way, shape or form. Ironically different is what will save this planet from extinction. Currently we will be a moment in history that will not even rival the dinosaurs. For all of our smarts we can't survive as well as beasts.

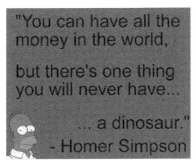

"You can have all the money in the world, but there's one thing you will never have... ... a dinosaur."
- Homer Simpson

The fact is that the sooner crazy becomes the accepted norm the better. Sometimes I pretend to be normal is what we are all doing most of the time and the answer to this planet and mankind's survival will be found by crazy individuals. There are two groups on this planet the first is a group that wants the whole of humanity equally to survive. The second is the group that sees the masses as expendable and having served their purpose will plan to save only themselves and others like them as they believe that they are special. Sadly, our governments and leaders are largely made up from the second group. Any resistance will just bring more of the same into our lives. The wars on drugs, disease and terrorism have just attracted more of the same. As Mother Teresa said when asked to attend an anti-war march. Something to the tune of - "Ask me when you hold a pro-peace march." The difference is subtle but it is vital when it comes to creating our realities. Be **for** what you want not against the opposite.

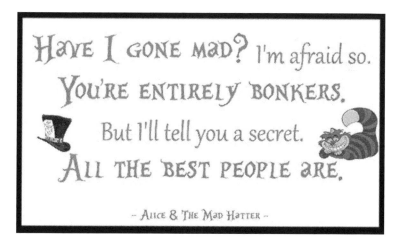

I am rooting for the first group and the evolution of more of that group to take themselves away from the small minded "special"

people. There is no getting away from the fact that we as human beings are becoming more connected and loving in one group and less connected and more fearful in the other group. Which group will evolve? The "special" group may just be too busy distracted, amassing more stuff and winning to realise that they are losing their connection to source and are stuck in their greed whilst humanity evolves around them. I think the time has come to stop pretending to be normal and realise that we are all exceptional and our task is to boost the power of love in this world to such an extent that nothing can exist in opposition. It is time to use our imaginations, time we tell the story of how we want it to be and just watch it happen, making the right choices when we are called upon and living in service to each other from dawn till dusk.

I have decided that crazy is far worthier than normal. No more pretending.

Peace and Love

x Adam x

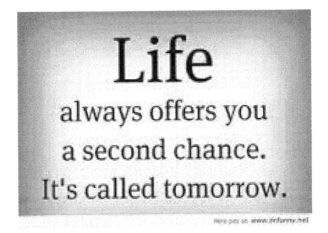

# Getting Better

**Top Personal Development Books**

**www.adamsenex.com**

**Top Personal Development Blog @**

**www.MoreRebelThanZen.com**

**Life Coaching @ www.soul2whole.com**

 **Adam Senex – Getting Better Series**

Book 1 – Dazed & Confused

Book 2 – More Rebel Than Zen

Book 3 – Chilled Demons Cheeky Heroes

Book 4 – Sometimes I Pretend To Be Normal

Book 5 – Coming Soon……..

# also

The Great Body Bible - The Fitness Wizards
available from www.authorhouse.co.uk

Feeding The Active Body - Gary Walsh

Made in the USA
Charleston, SC
01 August 2016